JAPAN

*from Shogun
to Sony
1543-1984*

Books by John R. Roberson

John R. Roberson

JAPAN

from Shogun to Sony
1543-1984

*illustrated with photographs,
prints and maps*

ATHENEUM

New York

To Charlene, David and Kathryn Roberson

Library of Congress Cataloging in Publication Data

Roberson, John R.
Japan from Shogun to Sony.

"Illustrated by photographs & prints."
Bibliography.
Includes index.
SUMMARY: Presents the history of Japan from the arrival of the first
Europeans in the sixteenth century to its mid-twentieth century
development into a leading industrial nation.
1. Japan—History—Tokugawa period, 1600-1868—Juvenile
literature. 2. Japan—History 1868-   —Juvenile literature.
[1. Japan—History—Tokugawa period, 1600-1868.
2. Japan—History—1868-   ] I. Title.
DS871.R63 1985   952'.025   84-21622
ISBN 0-689-31076-5

Atheneum
Macmillan Publishing Company
866 Third Avenue, New York, NY 10022
Collier Macmillan Canada, Inc.

Composition by Heritage Press, Charlotte, North Carolina
Printed and bound by Fairfield Graphics, Inc., Fairfield, Pennsylvania

First Edition

3 5 7 9 11 13 15 17 19 F/C 20 18 16 14 12 10 8 6 4

Acknowledgments

First I would like to thank those individual Japanese who have taken a helpful interest in this work: Hironaka Wakako of Tokyo for permission to quote from a speech she gave at Yale University; Iwanaga Yukiko of Tokyo and Niwano Yoshihiro of Sagamihara for valuable guidance in research; and Harada Michio, Vice Consul of Japan in New York, and Wajima Masakatsu of the Japan Information Center for assistance with illustrations.

The New York Public Library's Research Library and Mid-Manhattan Library; the Greenwich Library; the Perrot Library, Old Greenwich, CT and the indispensable Interlibrary Loan Service have supplied me with most of the books in the bibliography and are all worthy of the status, as the Japanese would put it, of National Treasure.

Finally, I would like to thank Marjorie Baldini of Briarcliff Manor, N.Y., and Felix Cayo of Los Angeles for first suggesting, independently of each other, that I follow up my *China from Manchu to Mao* with a similar book on Japan.

Contents

Glossary

bushido. The code of behavior for samurai; literally, "the way of the warrior."

daimyo. A lord who had much land and many samurai warriors; literally, "great lord."

Diet. The Japanese legislature.

Exclusion Acts. Decrees of the shogun in the seventeenth century forbidding the Japanese foreign trade and travel.

hara-kiri. A word for ritual suicide, used for the more proper term, *seppuku.* Literally, "belly cutting."

kabuki. The lively popular theater of Japan.

MITI. The Ministry for International Trade and Industry, the influential government bureau of economic experts who advise companies about desirable national objectives.

noh. The stately theater of Japan originally intended for the nobility.

ronin. samurai warriors with no master.

samurai. The warrior class in feudal Japan, ranking just below the nobility. Samurai rank continued to be passed from father to son long after samurai skills were supplanted by modern warfare.

seppuku. Ritual suicide by cutting the abdomen.

shogun. A title given to the strongest military man in Japan. The shoguns ruled the country in the name of the emperor from 1192 to 1868.

ukiyo-e. Wood-block prints depicting the "floating world"—sections of Japanese cities devoted to entertainment.

zaibatsu. One of the huge corporations that owned most of Japanese industry, particularly in the years before World War II. Literally, "financial clique."

A note on language

The Japanese write their names with family name first and given name second. That practice is followed throughout this book. Given names of boys often end in -ro or -o. Given names of girls often end in -ko or -e.

Consonants are usually pronounced with the vowel that follows them: *roku*, six, is ro-ku (not rok-u), *ikutsu*, how many, is i-ku-tsu (not ik-ut-su). The vowels u and i are dropped in pronouncing some words: *suki* is ski, *desu* is des, *shita* is shta, Matsushita is Ma-tsu-shta. Each syllable of a word receives almost equal stress.

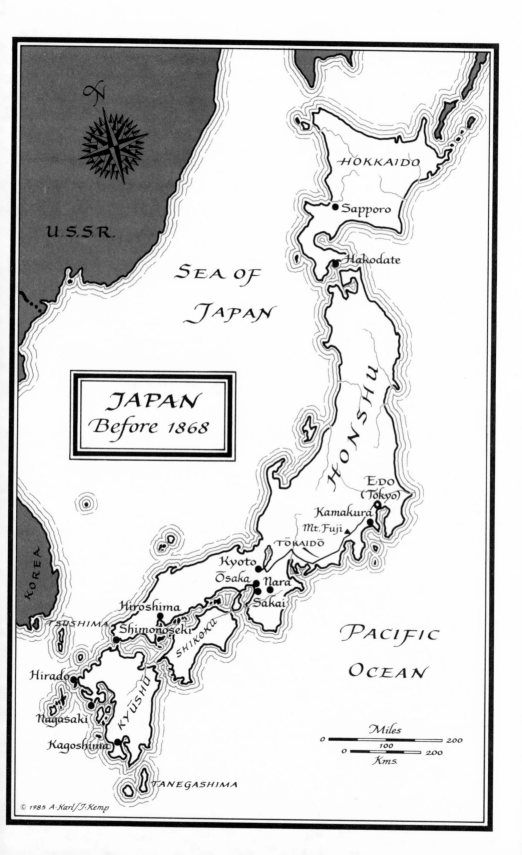

N

U.S.S.R.

SEA OF

JAPAN

HOKKAIDO

• Sapporo

• Hakodate

JAPAN
Before 1868

HONSHU

EDO
(Tokyo)

Kamakura
Mt. Fuji

TŌKAIDŌ

Kyoto
Ōsaka
Nara
Sakai

Hiroshima

Shimonoseki

SHIKOKU

KOREA

TSUSHIMA

Hirado

PACIFIC

OCEAN

KYŪSHŪ

Nagasaki

Kagoshima

TANEGASHIMA

Miles
0   100   200
0   100   200
Kms.

© 1985 A·Karl/J·Kemp

Round Eyes
in Japan

 On September 23, 1543, word came to the ruler of a small Japanese island that a ship had arrived offshore, carrying a number of strange-looking men from a distant country. According to their interpreter, they were traders who had come "in the hope of exchanging what they have for what they do not have."

The ruler, whose name was Lord Tokitaka, sent a small fleet of boats to escort the ship into harbor. Many traders had visited his realm, because of its location at the southern tip of the chain of islands that make up the nation of Japan, and he and his people had profited from their visits. But these men, according to the report, looked very different from any seen before. What they had to offer was also different. One item was especially remarkable.

"Two leaders among the traders," an eyewitness wrote later, "carried in their hands something two or three feet long,

The Portuguese ships that began to visit Japan in 1543 were the largest craft ever seen in the Orient. Japanese artists painted many pictures of these ships and the strange "barbarians" who sailed in them.

straight on the outside with a passage inside, and made of a heavy substance. To use it, fill it with powder and small lead pellets. Set up a target. Grip the object in your hand, compose your body, and closing one eye, apply fire to the aperture. Then the pellet hits the target squarely. The explosion is like lightning, and the report like thunder."

The remarkable object was a musket, or more precisely, a harquebus. The men, who looked so strange to the Japanese, were from Portugal, the European nation that had had the most success in establishing a trade by sea with the Orient. A Portuguese, Vasco da Gama, had been the first European to sail around the southern tip of Africa to India, in 1498. In the years since then, the Portuguese had explored more and more of the coast of Asia and the islands of the Pacific, establishing trading stations where they could. Now, in 1543, they had reached Japan.

Lord Tokitaka saw the harquebus demonstrated and said to the traders, "Incapable though I am, I should like to learn about it." They were, of course, happy to teach him. And on a public holiday the next month, they gave a public demonstration, firing at a target a hundred paces away. Lord Tokitaka's subjects were astonished, then frightened. But before long they also wanted to learn about the weapon. The ruler bought two samples at a high price and began diligent target practice. More important, he directed men who were skilled in working with iron to study the samples he had bought and learn to make such weapons themselves.

Half a century later, muskets were in use all over Japan. They changed warfare, and with it Japanese history. And the word the Japanese used for musket was Tanegashima—the name of Lord Tokitaka's island. As one of his descendants justly claimed, "Lord Tokitaka, with one volley of the weapon, startled sixty provinces of our country."

The Portuguese traders continued on their journey, elated. For some months a story had been circulating around the trading stations saying that three sailors in a small boat had been driven out to sea by a storm and been thrown up on the shore of a wonderful island, where a highly civilized people cared for them and helped them to return to the mainland. Surely, the story went, this must be part of the wealthy island nation called Japan, that Marco Polo had heard about on his visit to China nearly three centuries before. Nobody could be certain of the names of the three sailors, or the exact date in 1542 or 1543 when they landed—the first Europeans to set foot in Japan. Several sailors claimed the honor. But now the traders who sold the muskets could confirm that Japan really did exist, and its people were indeed hospitable, prosperous, and eager to trade with merchants from afar.

Their news created great excitement in the trading stations. For some years the Portuguese had been trying to exchange "what they had for what they did not have" with the richest nation in the Orient, China. They had made little progress, for two reasons. The emperor of China placed many restrictions on trade with foreign "barbarians." Second, the Chinese already had almost everything the Portuguese offered, so there was little incentive to trade.

Trade with Japan sounded like a much better prospect. Who was the ruler there? How strong was he? How did he feel about trade? What goods were the Japanese likely to buy and sell? The Portuguese collected every scrap of information they could from Asian sailors and merchants who had visited Japan, and sent more of their own ships to explore.

Japan was a nation made up of four large islands and many small ones. The large island farthest south was named Kyushu. Just north of it was the largest island, Honshu. These were the two most often visited by traders.

The question of who was the ruler of Japan had several answers. Lord Tokitaka, who bought the muskets, ruled his island. Other lords ruled other territories, much as barons and dukes ruled parts of Europe in feudal days. The European barons and dukes had knights to do their fighting; the Japanese lords had samurai—warriors with privileged status handed down from father to son. These great fighting men were armed with razor-sharp samurai swords, equal to the best swords made in Europe.

The lords who ruled the largest territories were called daimyo, meaning great lords. In the mid 1500s, the daimyo were constantly forming alliances to fight other groups of daimyo. But no individual was strong enough to win lasting control over other lords. Japan, therefore, had hundreds of rulers.

Japan also had an emperor. He was believed to be a direct descendant of the god and goddess who had created the islands of Japan many centuries before, and as such he was worthy of great respect. But he had even less power than the queen of England has today, and far less wealth. In fact, lack of funds had forced the current emperor to delay for several years the ceremonies to mark the beginning of his reign. A daimyo finally contributed the money for the ceremonies and received a handsome title in return—the power to confer titles was about the only power the emperor had.

Although the emperor had no army, he did have a commander-in-chief, called the shogun. That title had been given in 1192 to a general who was strong enough to win military control of all Japan for a time and wise enough to profess loyalty to the divine emperor. But the current shogun, the Portuguese learned, controlled only the area around the city where the emperor lived, Kyoto, on the island of Honshu.

In sum, Japan was ruled by dozens of daimyo. Each daimyo ruled his own land pretty much as he liked, free from interference by emperor or shogun. Those daimyo who saw an opportunity to profit from trade with foreigners were free to do so.

What goods were the Japanese likely to buy? It was apparent that they were well supplied with the three necessities: food, clothing and shelter. They were skillful farmers, one Portuguese captain reported, growing wheat, barley, turnips, radishes, beets, beans, cucumbers, rice, yams, onions and other vegetables, and melons and other fruits. The clothes they wore were as good as anything worn in Portugal: sturdy cottons and woolens for ordinary people and silks and brocades for the nobles. They lived in houses of wood, skillfully constructed and kept in a state of cleanliness that astonished visitors from sixteenth-century Europe. And they built castles of huge stone blocks, precisely hewn and fitted together. Clearly these highly civilized people would have no interest in the shiny trinkets that delighted the simpler natives of some of the other islands the Portuguese had visited. Yet they showed a charming curiosity about everything foreign, very unlike the haughty Chinese. Where was Portugal? How did the Portuguese build such large ships, larger than any built in the Orient? Did they have charts showing the routes they sailed? The Japanese already knew about the compass, which the Chinese had invented about the eleventh century. But

Samurai warriors, guided by a strong code of honor and armed with two razor-sharp swords and a lance, were some of the most effective fighting men of all time.

were there other European inventions as intriguing as the musket?

On the other hand, the Japanese had plenty of goods to sell: magnificent sharp swords, lustrous pearls, quantities of gold, beautiful works of art, and more ordinary items like lumber and sulphur. They had been trading for centuries with other countries in the Orient, especially China and Korea. They recognized that certain Chinese products really were what the Chinese proudly claimed, the best in the world, and they were willing to pay to get the best. The Portuguese needed to find a way to supply the Japanese with the things they wanted (in addition to muskets), if they were to carry on trade.

Within a few years, a way presented itself. In 1548, the emperor of China insisted on the enforcement of a long-ignored decree that forbade Chinese subjects to trade with Japan. Chaos resulted. Many families living along the coast of China earned their livelihood from that trade. They turned to smuggling. Pirates raided coastal towns and carried off booty to sell in Japan, for merchants in Japan were willing to buy Chinese goods from anyone. But smugglers were sometimes caught and their goods confiscated by Chinese officials, and pirate ships were sometimes sunk or captured by other pirates. The merchants wanted a more dependable source of Chinese goods. Portugal provided it. The large Portuguese ships, with their huge sails and European weapons, could outrun and outfight any Oriental ship. The Portuguese traders began to buy goods in China to sell in Japan. This system was so successful that soon many daimyo in southern Japan were competing with each other to persuade Portuguese captains to come to their ports. The Portuguese government felt it necessary to regulate this profitable trade and soon allowed only one or two of Portugal's "great ships" to sail from China to Japan each year. But each voyage delivered cargo worth a fortune in Japan—double or even quadruple what the Portuguese had paid for it in China.

Trade was not the only purpose of the Portuguese voyages to Asia. The king of Portugal felt he had a responsibility to teach the Christian religion to the peoples there. In 1539, he had sent a request for help in this effort to Rome to the Pope. Specifically he had asked for missionaries from a group of men recently organized "to be the cavalry of the Church, ready to go anywhere at a moment's notice." This group took the name the Society of Jesus, and its members were called Jesuits. One of the members assigned to the Portuguese mission to the Orient was Francis Xavier, later to be known as St. Francis of the Indies.

For ten years, Francis Xavier traveled from island to island, converting thousands of people to Christianity. He was always on excellent terms with the captains and crews he sailed with. The stories the sailors told about Japan set him to thinking about opportunities for missionary work there. The people were intelligent, many could read and write, and they were receptive to new ideas. The power of Christianity, Francis Xavier was certain, would triumph over whatever religion they already had. He resolved to go to Japan as soon as he could find a way. When that opportunity did come, it came as the result of a combination of trade, religion and piracy.

In fact, the Japanese already had three religions. The oldest was Shinto, based on the belief that objects in nature— the moon, mountains, trees, even stones—contain spirits. The first emperor was the great-great-great-grandson of the sun goddess, who was in turn the daughter of the two deities who created the islands and people of Japan. Shinto asked little of believers beyond a few ceremonies at Shinto temples to show respect for the emperor and his divine ancestors.

The second religion was much more profound, based on the teaching of the Indian sage of the sixth century B.C., Gautama Buddha. Buddhism had spread from India to China to Korea to Japan. A short summation might be "well-being is achieved by freeing oneself from greed." By the 1500s, there

were a number of separate Buddhist groups in Japan, each
with its own temples and monasteries, trying to understand
fully what Buddha meant and how his goal might be achieved.

The third religion, Confucianism, was the most practical
of the three. It was based on the teaching of the Chinese sage,
Confucius, of the fifth century B.C. Confucius taught that the
well-being of a nation and its people depends on right rela-
tionships between all its parts—between parents and children,
between citizens and local rulers, between local rulers and
provincial rulers and so on right up to the emperor. In his
many sayings, he sought to show just what those right relation-
ships are, in various situations. Japanese followers of Confucius studied his sayings diligently, memorizing his words and
discussing their meaning.

Shinto, Buddhism and Confucianism recognized no deity
anything like the God Francis Xavier taught about, a god
who was still actively involved in the affairs of the world He
had created. But, in 1547, God took a hand in the conversion
of Japan, Francis Xavier believed. He sent the missionary a
young Japanese helper.

The young man's name was Anjiro. He lived in one of the
southern ports of Japan visited by the Portuguese and was so
interested in these foreigners that he learned some of their
language and listened to talk of their religion. He asked the
merchants and sailors questions that were too deep for them
to answer, and they told him about the remarkable priest,
Francis Xavier. One captain, Jorge Alvarez—it was he who
noted so carefully the vegetables grown in Japan—agreed to
take Anjiro on board his ship to the Portuguese trading station
at Malacca on the Malay Peninsula. Almost all ships stopped
there en route from India to the Pacific and back. Francis
Xavier was likely to stop there in time.

Captain Alvarez's prediction was correct. The priest arrived, and Alvarez presented Anjiro to him. Francis Xavier
had as many questions to ask as Anjiro. He requested the captain to write down everything he knew about Japan. And he

The Jesuit missionary Francis Xavier, now known as Saint Francis of the Indies, arrived in Japan in 1549, just six years after the first European merchants.

talked earnestly with Anjiro, who by this time spoke Portuguese "tolerably well," Xavier said, having no doubt put the weeks of the voyage to use practicing with the sailors. The priest was delighted. He wrote, "If all the Japanese are as eager to learn as Anjiro is, they are of all nations newly discovered most curious." In addition, Anjiro could act as interpreter for him in Japan. Surely the opportunity he had been waiting for had arrived.

While Francis Xavier made preparations to travel to Japan with two other Jesuits, Anjiro studied Christianity. He was baptized on Pentecost Sunday, 1548, with the Christian name Paul of the Faith. In the spring of 1549, the four men were ready to set out for Anjiro's home city, Kagoshima, on the island of Kyushu. But they found no Portuguese ship in Malacca that was headed that way. The only offer they had came from a well-known pirate whose Chinese junk was anchored in the harbor. After much discussion with the Portuguese governor of Malacca, and many prayers, Francis Xavier decided to entrust their lives and their mission to this craft and its daring captain. The pirate was good as his word and delivered them safe in Kagoshima on August 15, 1549.

The missionaries were well received by the lord of Anjiro's province, and by the lords of most of the neighboring provinces. The Jesuits had good European educations and much knowledge to impart. The Japanese were especially interested in what the priests told them about astronomy. The Jesuits were most interested, of course, in talking about religion. The Japanese listened politely as Anjiro interpreted the Jesuits' words. Some of the lords gave permission for their subjects to accept Christianity, and hundreds did. Some lords went even further and ordered their subjects to become Christians. But here we must consider another factor besides the eloquence of the missionaries.

The Japanese noticed at once that the Portuguese sailors and merchants who came to Japan showed great respect for these courageous priests who had made the long journey from Europe for the sake of their religion. Even rough seadogs who had not been inside a church in years treated them with courtesy. Clearly the Jesuits were men of considerable influence. Some of the lords hoped that if they helped the missionaries make converts, the missionaries would feel an obligation to them and direct profitable trade to their ports.

The Japanese noticed that the European merchants paid great respect to the early missionaries. That helped the priests win an audience for the message of Christianity.

Francis Xavier was a man of great vision, devoted to carrying out as much as he could the commission of his Savior: "Go ye therefore and teach all nations, baptizing them." He intended to baptize the whole nation of Japan if he could, and then go on to his next goal, converting the emperor of China. In the fall of 1550, he left Anjiro and one of the Jesuits to continue work on the island of Kyushu, and he set out with his other colleague for the nation's capital, Kyoto, on the central island of Honshu. He intended to speak to the emperor of Japan and to his commander-in-chief, the shogun, about Christianity. He found, however, that conditions on Honshu were quite different from those on Kyushu. The lords of Kyushu were principally interested in making money.

While they fought among themselves sometimes, they never fought for long, and then went back to peaceful trade. The lords of Honshu seemed just the opposite. They were chiefly interested in gaining power through waging war against other lords, and now, halfway through the sixteenth century, they had exhausted nearly all their resources in wars that had been going on for decades. They had many good ports, but few European ships visited them, so the Jesuits could find no friendly captain to take them to the port closest to Kyoto. They had to make their way on their own, on foot. They did so, walking two months in wintry weather.

When they arrived in Kyoto, they found that the shogun was away from the city, and the emperor had no interest in seeing two priests of a strange religion from a faraway country. Even Francis Xavier's remarkable effectiveness preaching to the man in the street faltered in wartorn Kyoto, where few stopped to listen to his sermons delivered in elementary Japanese, without the help of an interpreter. The two Jesuits concluded, realistically, that their efforts were more fruitful in Kyushu, and they returned there. The following November, Francis Xavier left the work in Japan in the hands of the two other Jesuits and Anjiro and set out for China. He died there a year later.

Other Jesuits arrived in Japan, and in the next twenty years the influence of their mission increased. Some Japanese became such devoted Christians that when later rulers ordered them to renounce their faith, they chose to die instead. Others kept Christianity alive in secret from generation to generation for two hundred years. There can be no doubt about the sincerity of their beliefs. But neither can there be any doubt that some Japanese still hoped the Jesuits would bring them commerce.

The lord of a province on the west coast of Kyushu thought of a way to turn these hopes into reality. The Jesuits wanted to set up a permanent headquarters for their missionary activities in Japan. This lord offered them a quantity of land beside an excellent harbor, protected from storms by a circle of hills. There was only a little fishing village there then, named Nagasaki. His only conditions were that the great ships come to Nagasaki each year and pay an annual fee of one thousand ducats, most of which would be used for the support of the Jesuit priests. The Jesuits reported the offer to the Portuguese merchants. The harbor was very suitable for the great ships, and everyone was pleased with the offer except the lords of the rival provinces. Within five years the village had grown to a town of thirty thousand people, and in time it became the chief city of Kyushu.

In the twenty-five years following the arrival of the first Portuguese merchants with their muskets, the Europeans brought about significant changes in Japan. Their ships greatly increased the foreign trade of the nation. Their missionaries introduced a strong new element into its religious life. Then, in the twenty-fifth year, 1568, their firearms helped a Japanese general to gain control of the nation's capital and lay the foundation for the first strong central government Japan had had for two centuries. And that general had strong opinions about foreigners. His name was Oda Nobunaga.

Two Young Rulers
in Samurai Days

 Oda Nobunaga was born in 1534, about ninety miles east of the emperor's capital city of Kyoto. As a boy he enjoyed exploring the beautiful mountains and valleys around his home. Members of the Oda family had served as minor officials of their province for several generations, and Nobunaga's father expanded his lands and influence enough to become known in Kyoto as a leader in his province. Then, when Nobunaga was seventeen, his father died. He had named Nobunaga his heir and head of the family. Because of his youth, some of his relatives tried to deny him that rank, but the young man raised a small army of about a thousand foot soldiers and defeated all his rivals. By the time he was twenty-five, he was not only head of the family, but also the master of all his province. That year, he traveled to the capital, where he was warmly received by the shogun, who was always looking for help in maintaining his shaky control over the provinces around the capital.

The next year, 1560, Nobunaga learned that the lord of
a large province to the east was leading an army of twenty-
five thousand men to attack Kyoto. He had to cross Nobunaga's province to reach the capital. Soon Nobunaga lost
two forts to the advancing army. Although his own army was
only about three thousand men, Nobunaga decided to counterattack. The knowledge of the terrain that he had gained
as a boy served him well. The invaders camped in a narrow
gorge to rest and eat the midday meal. Nobunaga knew that
a large army could not use its full force in such a small space.
He led his men there. At that point the weather took a hand,
as it has in many historic battles. A sudden heavy rainstorm
hit the little valley and turned the camp to mud. When the
rain stopped, Nobunaga struck. The invaders, taken completely by surprise, picked their swords and spears from the
mud. But their deadliest weapons, newly acquired muskets,
were soaked and would not fire. The invading lord was slain
in the fighting. Kyoto was saved, and Nobunaga's reputation
spread throughout Japan.

Nobunaga, twenty-six years old, now saw that he might
be much more than lord of his native province. He could
aspire to be leader of the whole region. Other provincial
lords had succeeded in doing that. The western end of
Honshu, consisting of twelve provinces, was dominated by
one great lord, and the rich plain in eastern Honshu (where
Tokyo now stands) by another. Southern Kyushu was dominated by another. These men had gained their power not so
much by the strength of their own armies as by their success
in putting together "alliances." One lord would propose to
another that the two of them ask a third to join them in an
alliance. The members of the alliance would enjoy the protection of the combined strength of the whole. But if a lord
declined the invitation, the alliance would take his lands by
force and divide them among the members. An alliance was
held together by the double desire for protection and for
seized lands. But there was nothing to prevent a member
from switching to another alliance, if he thought it to his

Oda Nobunaga, born in 1534, inherited leadership of his clan when he was seventeen. By the time he was thirty-four, he was the most powerful man in Japan, and was invited by the emperor to help enforce his imperial decrees.

advantage. To help make sure that his new alliance was stronger than his old, he might not tell his old allies his plans and simply turn up at a crucial battle fighting on the other side. Such treachery changed the outcome of many battles in Japan.

Nobunaga began to build such a regional alliance, which he hoped would someday expand to dominate Kyoto. In the next seven years, he made alliances with the lords of three other provinces, and when a fourth rejected the invitation to join them, they conquered his province. In the meantime, in Kyoto, the shogun had been murdered by followers of another ambitious lord. The shogun's younger brother asked Nobunaga to help him become shogun, and soon the emperor also asked Nobunaga for help. Nobunaga placed on his shield a new motto, "Rule the Empire by Force," and led his men, joined by the soldiers of his allies, toward Kyoto. He overcame all opposition along the way and entered the capital in triumph in 1568.

Nobunaga paid great respect to the emperor, whose divine approval was necessary for his plans. He also allowed the murdered shogun's younger brother to be named the new shogun; but when Nobunaga found the man was plotting against him, he declared the post vacant. Nobunaga did not claim the title for himself, but it was obvious that he was in fact the emperor's "commander-in-chief." He proceeded to increase the number of provinces under his control, sometimes by alliance, sometimes by conquest. In another of his historic battles, fought in 1575 at Nagashino, against the lord of an eastern province, he showed how well he understood that the nature of warfare had changed. It was no longer a glorious contest between knights on horseback. Nobunaga built a sort of wooden stockade on the battle line, too high for a horse to jump over, and placed men with muskets behind it. Four successive cavalry charges attacked this position and suffered heavy casualties. This broke the force of the enemy's attack and the victory was Nobunaga's.

Another enemy understood the use of the musket much better. That enemy was a group of militant Buddhist monks. In the centuries since Buddhism first came to Japan, that religion had separated into many different sects. Some of these had become very wealthy and had built splendid temples and universities. To protect their treasures, they had also trained their own armies. In time, some of their religious buildings were more like fortresses than temples. Mightiest of all these was the "cathedral" of Honganji, near the port city of Osaka, twenty-five miles south of Kyoto. The monks there had recognized the power of the musket very early and had set up their own arsenal. By the time Nobunaga sought to rule Japan, they were well-armed with the new weapons. This particular sect had been attracting followers in great numbers in many provinces. Its leaders were as determined as Nobunaga to "rule the empire" in their own way.

When Nobunaga saw that these Buddhist leaders would not help him, but on the contrary were urging their followers to help his enemies, he sent his soldiers to destroy the mon-

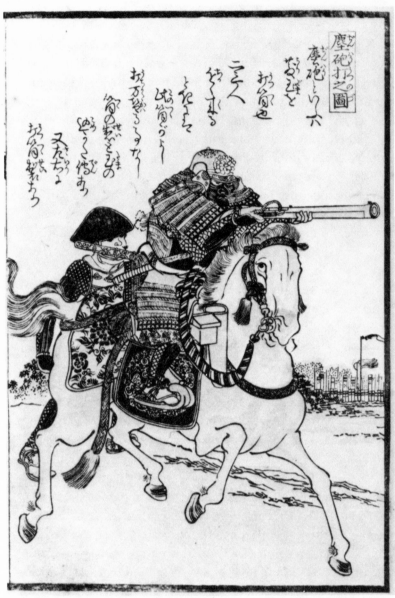

Oda Nobunaga was one of the first Japanese generals to understand the power of Western firearms in battle. These pictures are from a manual he commissioned on the subject.

asteries and kill the monks. This was easily accomplished at
the ancient monasteries on the mountains around Kyoto,
where the buildings were burned and thousands of persons—
monks and their followers—were slain. But it took eleven
years to conquer the cathedral fortress of Honganji near
Osaka. The monks there surrendered only after a long siege
cut off their sources of supplies.

The Europeans naturally watched Nobunaga's rise to power
with great interest and some anxiety. What would be his attitude toward their trade and missionary activities? Things
were going well for them on the south island, Kyushu. They
were beginning to make progress on the central island,
Honshu. European ships were welcomed there, and a few
Jesuits were allowed to preach, even in the capital. If the
Europeans could win Nobunaga's friendship, they might
greatly expand their activities.

In 1569, the year after Nobunaga gained control of Kyoto,
a Christian daimyo arranged for him to receive one of the
Jesuit missionaries, Luis Frois. The timing of the meeting
could not have been better. That day Nobunaga was engaged in one of the activities he enjoyed most, building a new
castle. He was supervising the work himself, dressed in rough
clothes and a tiger-skin cloak. Some of the stone for the castle
had come from the demolition of shrines of Buddhist sects
that had opposed him. Frois and Nobunaga soon found a common ground for conversation in criticizing the Buddhists.
Nobunaga sent the priest on an inspection tour of the construction site and invited him to visit him again. Frois was delighted to accept. In time, Nobunaga granted the Jesuits his
official permission to preach in Japan, which enraged the
Buddhists, as he knew it would. He even gave the Jesuits land
near his own favorite castle to build a school and visited them
there. The Jesuit Gaspar Coelho reported:

> A few days ago Nobunaga came unexpectedly to our
> house. He doubtless wished to take them by surprise

so that he could inspect the cleanliness and neatness of our houses, because he is a great enemy of dirt and disorder. As Father Organtino knows his views on this point, Nobunaga found nothing to criticize. He began to talk to the Fathers and Brothers with much affection and familiarity. He went along to look at the clock, and he also saw a harpsichord and viol which we have in the house. He had them both played and took great delight in listening to their music; he highly praised the boy who played the harpsichord and also commended the boy who played the viol. After that he went to see the bell and other curious things which the Fathers keep in that house. When he arrived back [at his castle], he sent Father Organtino a present of things to eat, with a message saying that he had much enjoyed visiting his house that day and that he was sending the gift as a token of his great pleasure.

The Jesuits' religion, however, impressed Nobunaga not at all. According to Father Frois, "He openly proclaims that there are no such things as a Creator of the Universe nor immortality of the soul, nor any life after death." He was willing for priests—Buddhist or Christian—to educate the people and discuss philosophy. But if they opposed him, as the militant Buddhists had, he crushed them cruelly. His cruelty probably did not surprise the Jesuits, accustomed to the bloody religious wars of Europe.

European merchants also enjoyed Nobunaga's favor. For him, trade was a means to wealth, and wealth was a means to power. He saw that there was a lot of money to be made from the goods brought from China in the Portuguese ships. He encouraged the trade. Business flourished. With the surrender of the cathedral fortress near Osaka, in 1580, it seemed Nobunaga's control of the heart of Japan was complete. The next year he held a great parade, in which twenty thousand horsemen from the seven provinces around Kyoto rode past the emperor's reviewing stand. It was an impressive display.

The lords of about a third of Japan's sixty-six provinces acknowledged Nobunaga's power. A third was not enough. He wanted to rule all the empire: his dream of a unified Japan was his greatest contribution to history. He continued his efforts to make alliances with other lords and to subdue by force those who rejected him.

In 1582, one of his best generals, named Hideyoshi, was engaged in a campaign to subdue the twelve allied provinces on the western end of the island of Honshu. Hideyoshi, who began his military career as a common foot soldier, was a man of great ability, rarely at a loss for a solution to a problem, as he was to demonstrate many times in the years ahead. When a key castle in the west resisted his attacks, he built dikes to divert the water of a river to flood it. The danger to the castle caused the western alliance to send a strong force to its defense.

It was at this moment that one of Nobunaga's allies decided to turn traitor. He and his men surrounded Nobunaga's quarters, overwhelmed his fierce resistance, and set fire to the building. Nobunaga and his eldest son both perished. The traitor seized a quantity of the dead man's silver and set about using it to try to buy allies in the leaderless days that followed.

When Hideyoshi received the news that his master was dead, he calmly kept it a secret and suggested to the daimyo of the west that they talk peace. The daimyo, believing all Nobunaga's might was still behind Hideyoshi, agreed to surrender three provinces and the flooded castle. The next day Hideyoshi headed for the capital to deal with the traitorous ally, whom he defeated in battle just nine days after the death of Nobunaga. Having avenged his master's death, he called a meeting of Nobunaga's allies to choose a successor, since the eldest son was dead.

The historian George Sansom describes the meeting:

> Nobunaga's second and third son began to quarrel, and the discussion floundered until Hideyoshi, with

Hideyoshi succeeded in unifying all Japan under his just rule. He began his career as a common foot soldier, too poor to have more than a single name.

his usual practical wisdom, went into an adjoining room and came back holding in his arms the infant grandson of Nobunaga (the son of his first-born), who was at once declared the heir.

The allies agreed to form a council to govern for the child. But the practical effect of the choice, as Hideyoshi no doubt foresaw, was that one strongest general would soon rule in Nobunaga's place.

There was only one general in Japan who might be Hideyoshi's match: Tokugawa Ieyasu. He had also fought long and well for Nobunaga, subduing provinces to the east of Kyoto while Hideyoshi was winning victories to the west. When he received the news of Nobunaga's death, he went at once to his own province, to strengthen his army in order to avenge his master—and perhaps seize power himself. After Hideyoshi's quick success in Kyoto, Hideyoshi sent word to Ieyasu that his help was not needed, and Ieyasu decided to continue building up his strength and await developments.

Two years later Ieyasu fought two battles against Hideyoshi, both of which he seemed about to win when Hideyoshi proposed terms for peace. After some months of confrontation, the two recognized they could accomplish more by cooperation than by killing each other's troops, and Ieyasu became Hideyoshi's strongest ally.

Together, the two generals had a strength no lord could resist. In 1586, the emperor granted Hideyoshi the title chancellor, thus giving him his blessing. By 1590, every lord in Japan had pledged allegiance to Hideyoshi. The system of alliances that had given Nobunaga control of twenty provinces, now covered all sixty-six provinces of Japan. But even as his control spread, Hideyoshi knew that any of the lords could be looking for ways to escape from his domination. He must prevent that.

His first tactic was simple, direct and traditional in Japan. He insisted that the great regional daimyo send him as hostages their wives, their heirs, and certain important men from their provinces. All these Hideyoshi treated as his guests, but they were hostages nonetheless, not free to return to their homes.

Second, Hideyoshi saw to it that the daimyo shared in the spoils of his victory. Those spoils were enormous, drawn from the wealth of an entire nation. He went about dividing them up in a systematic fashion. He ordered a new survey of all the farmland in Japan. Each piece of land was registered in the name of the family who tilled it, along with an estimate of how much rice it could produce. A number of farms were grouped together as a village, and the village was assessed a tax based on estimated total production. Every daimyo who pledged allegiance to Hideyoshi was assigned a number of villages. He was responsible for governing them and collecting the tax. Part of the tax he used to pay his soldiers and the officials who helped him govern. The rest was his to keep.

The richest lands, and a number of the major cities—

Kyoto, Sakai, Nagasaki and others—Hideyoshi assigned to himself. At the time of his death, the estimated total rice production of Japan was 92.5 million bushels; of this, 10 million bushels, or nearly eleven percent, came from lands under Hideyoshi's direct control. The effect of the land survey and the accompanying taxation was to institute in Japan a new feudal system, similar to the feudal system in Europe in the Middle Ages. The peasants who grew the food kept only a part. The rest went to the daimyo.

Hideyoshi was the son of a peasant. He knew that the peasants would resent the system. That led to the third of the actions he took to ensure the continuation of his rule: a nationwide "sword hunt." Throughout Japanese history, the local lords had raised armies by recruiting able-bodied men from the farms, who fought until a war was over and then went back to growing food. The recruits brought with them whatever weapons they had and took them home again. Hideyoshi knew the peasants had sometimes banded together in effective rebellions. Therefore, he required every household to turn in any weapons it had. To make his sword hunt a bit more acceptable to the people, he announced that the weapons would all be melted down to make nails and bolts for a temple he was building in Kyoto to house a huge new image of Buddha. Contributing their weapons to this project, he said, would assure the peasants salvation in this world and the next.

By these three methods, Hideyoshi maintained his control of Japan for sixteen years. He and the daimyo collected great riches, which they spent with zest. Castles were their passion. The primary purpose of a castle, of course, is military, to control places of strategic importance in warfare. But those built in Hideyoshi's time had economic and cultural effects as well. A typical castle contained the residence of the daimyo and his chief vassals. The soldiers of the daimyo were quartered just outside the walls, in a garrison town. Here the daimyo built a temple or temples, and here mer-

1. Le Château.
2. La Ville.
3. Le Pont de pierre.
4. Le Palanquin de notre Ambassadeur.
5. Le Capitaine de la garde de l'Empereur.
6. Le Gouverneur.
7. Le Commissaire General.
8. La Douane.

La ville d'Oenewarrim
de la riviere

Japanese rulers of the sixteenth and seventeenth centuries loved to build castles. This picture by a French artist shows a castle on a bluff and the necessary farms, shops, temples and barracks nearby.

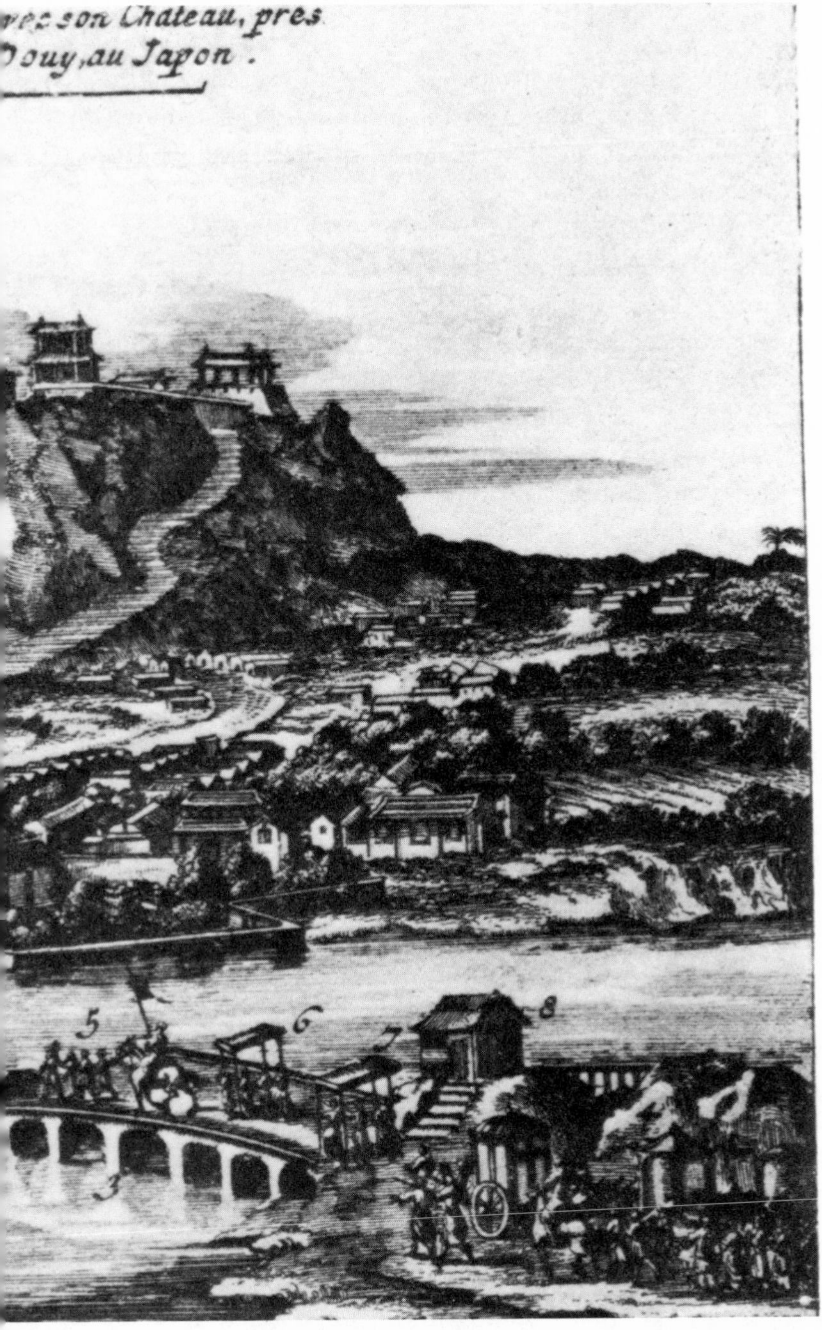

...vec son Chateau, pres
...Douy, au Japon.
5
6
7
8
3

chants and craftsmen set up shops to supply the castle and the soldiers. Beyond the town were the fields that provided food. In a comparatively short time, many of these castle towns grew into important cities.

Hideyoshi chose to build his principal castle at the town of Osaka, where the river Yodo, which passes near Kyoto, flows into the sea. Anyone who thought to attack Kyoto from the west would have to march up the Yodo Valley. In addition, Osaka was just a few miles from the great commercial city of Sakai, a major source of Hideyoshi's income. In time, the castle town at Osaka grew larger than Sakai, and is today the second largest city in Japan.

So much building activity meant prosperity for the artists and craftsmen who supplied decoration and furnishings for the many new residences, and clothes for the lords and officials. Hideyoshi had been poor in his youth, and he enjoyed showing everybody that now he was rich. Many of the lords followed his example. The period is remembered for its lavish use of bright colors, its intricate carvings on pillars and panels, its folding screens covered with quantities of gold. This style is quite different from that of most Japanese crafts before and after, which strive for a more subtle and refined beauty, but it expressed the exuberance of the times.

Merchants also prospered, selling the wares of the craftsmen and also food for the increasing number of city dwellers who had left the farms. Since the merchants produced nothing themselves, but profited from the labor of others, they were considered the lowest class in society. The craftsmen ranked above them. The farmers, the basic source of the nation's wealth, were above the craftsmen. The top position was held by the samurai warriors, with their glorious tradition. Like the merchants, they produced nothing and were supported by the labor of others, but they had held a position of power in Japan for so long that few questioned their value—and none dared do so openly.

During Hideyoshi's rule, the great ship from China continued to make its annual visit to Nagasaki, since Hideyoshi, like Nobunaga before him, knew that trade meant wealth, and wealth meant power. The combination of Portuguese commerce with Jesuit missionary activity also continued, although Hideyoshi's announced policy toward Christianity changed several times. He assigned the Jesuits a site in Osaka to build a church and residence. In 1586, he granted them permission to preach throughout Japan. But the next year, he issued an edict saying that the Portuguese merchants must bring no more priests, and all Jesuits in Japan must leave within twenty days. The Jesuits, who numbered about 120, assembled in the domain of a Christian daimyo, who protected them until Hideyoshi was persuaded to change his mind once again.

For half a century the Portuguese merchants and the Jesuit priests had been almost the only Europeans to visit Japan. But sixteen hundred miles to the south, another European nation had been establishing its influence. Spain, at that time the most powerful nation in Europe, had sent ships from its colony in Mexico across the Pacific to the Philippine Islands. A profitable commerce had grown up. With the Spanish ships had come missionaries of the Franciscan order. The Franciscans knew of the success of the Jesuits in making converts to Christianity in Japan, and they longed to share in it. When the Spanish sent a group of Franciscans as ambassadors to Hideyoshi, he gave them permission to travel in Japan, provided they did not preach. But the Franciscans soon ignored this condition and began to build churches. Bad feeling soon developed between the Portuguese Jesuits and the Spanish Franciscans. The Portuguese feared that open disregard of Hideyoshi's orders would bring down his wrath on all Christians, while the Spanish thought the Portuguese too timid.

In 1597, an accident called the attention of Hideyoshi to the actions of the Franciscans. A Spanish ship, bound from Manila to Mexico, was blown ashore in Japan by a storm.

Some of Hideyoshi's officials urged the ruler to confiscate the goods on the ship. To give weight to the suggestion, they told him the details of the Spanish priests' disobedience of his orders. Adding fuel to the fire, when Hideyoshi sent men to take the ship, the ship's pilot warned that they should not anger mighty Spain and showed them a map of Spain's colonies around the world. The Japanese asked how one nation had acquired so much territory. The pilot's reply was disastrously frank: "Our kings begin by sending into the countries they wish to conquer missionaries who induce the people to embrace our religion, and when they have made considerable progress, troops are sent who combine with the new Christians, and then our kings have not much trouble in accomplishing the rest."

Hideyoshi was understandably furious when he heard this. He had long suspected that the Europeans' real reason for coming to Japan was just what the pilot said. Three Franciscans, seventeen of their converts, and three Japanese Jesuit priests were crucified—by the Japanese method, which nailed the victim to a tree, and then provided instant death by two spear thrusts. Hideyoshi also set about expelling the Portuguese Jesuits. But that was only one of many worries he had by 1597.

Hideyoshi's main concern, always, was the continuation of the system of alliances he had built up, the system that gave Japan a unified government. As each additional daimyo pledged allegiance to Hideyoshi, additional land and income was added to the system, to the benefit of all the others. The last major addition to the system was the fertile plain near present-day Tokyo, whose lord was forced to submit in 1590. This rich area Hideyoshi assigned to his strong rival-turned-ally, Tokugawa Ieyasu. That gave Ieyasu a handsome reward for his help, but it also took him well away from Kyoto, and well away from his native province where he had built up his military strength.

Once all Japan was part of the system, there were no more provinces Hideyoshi could promise the daimyo as rewards for their loyalty. Equally worrisome, there were thousands of warriors with no battles to fight. Hideyoshi thought he knew the solution. Japan's trade with China was still being handled by Portuguese merchants, since the Chinese emperor would not allow Japanese traders in his realm. Hideyoshi decided to invade China and force the emperor to change his mind.

The part of the Asiatic mainland closest to Japan is the peninsula of Korea, at that time a kingdom under the protection of China. Hideyoshi asked the king of Korea for permission for his armies to march across the peninsula on their way to China, and when the king refused, he ordered an attack on Korea. This was neither the first time nor the last that Korea would be a battleground in other nations' wars. The story has a very familiar sound to those who remember the history of the war in Korea in the 1950s, when armies from the United States and many other nations fought there. In May, 1592, Japanese troops landed at Pusan, in the south, and in less than three weeks they occupied Seoul, the capital. By July, some units had penetrated almost to the Yalu River, the boundary between Korea and China. They stopped to await orders.

Clearly the king of Korea had not expected an invasion. He sent an urgent request for help to the emperor of China. And, belatedly, he ordered the admiral of the excellent Korean navy to act. The Korean admiral soon established complete control of the situation on the sea, halting the ships bringing reinforcements and supplies for the invaders. That meant the Japanese soldiers in Korea—some one hundred and fifty thousand men—were, in effect, stranded. The emperor of China responded more slowly, sending a small force across the Yalu River, which the Japanese quickly defeated. Early the next year, a much larger Chinese army pushed the Japanese south and recaptured Seoul. Peace negotiations followed, which lasted for three years. Hideyoshi's generals disagreed in their estimates of prospects for success in influencing the Chinese emperor. But in 1597, Hideyoshi sent more troops to Korea, who joined the Japanese still holding on to the area around Pusan. They defeated the Chinese and the Koreans on several occasions. Then, before the fighting produced any significant results, Hideyoshi died, on September 18, 1598. The invaders returned home to Japan.

The adventure in Korea had failed in its announced purpose, to open China to Japanese trade. But it had kept Japan's military men occupied, and Hideyoshi's system of alliances still covered all of Japan at the time of his death. The construction of a united nation was an achievement that has earned lavish praise for the son of a simple family. The British historian James Murdoch called him "the greatest statesman of his century, whether in Japan or Europe." And George Sansom wrote, "It is usually agreed that Hideyoshi is the greatest man in the history of Japan." As a general, his brilliance won many victories, but he disliked killing, and rarely took revenge on his enemies. He was friendly with people of all ranks. Although many grumbled at his nationwide land survey and attempted to escape from the taxation that accompanied it, it was fair and just. Without question, the stable, effective government Hideyoshi established gave the Japanese people a security and prosperity greater than they had known for centuries.

3
A Government
Built to Last

 "Nobunaga mixed the dough. Hideyoshi baked the cake. Ieyasu ate it." So goes an old Japanese saying, summarizing the way three powerful generals made a unified nation of the sixty-six provinces of Japan. Shortly before Hideyoshi died, he asked a council of lords, which included his strongest ally, Tokugawa Ieyasu, to promise to protect his five-year-old son until the child was old enough to rule. They promised. But rule by a council acting in the name of a child had not worked in the case of Nobunaga's heir in 1582, and it did not work after the death of Hideyoshi in 1598. The alliance Hideyoshi had put together soon broke apart. Ieyasu was now the strongest man in Japan. He proved it by defeating a group of rivals in the Battle of Sekigahara, fought on October 20, 1600. More important, Ieyasu saw that the nation needed a government built on a foundation more lasting than the power of one man. He created a government that lasted more than two-and-a-half centuries.

Tokugawa Ieyasu was the first member of the Tokugawa family to earn the title shogun—the emperor's "barbarian-subduing commander-in-chief." He founded a form of government that lasted Japan for two hundred sixty-four years.

In 1603, the emperor gave Ieyasu the title shogun. That title had been given in 1192 to the emperor's strongest general. Since 1192, the power of a few great families had made the post almost hereditary, handed down from generation to generation. But after the long civil wars of 1500s, neither emperor nor shogun had any real strength. Nobunaga had been the emperor's strongest general, in fact, not in title. When the man who had inherited the title shogun defied him, Nobunaga deposed him and declared the post vacant. With Ieyasu named shogun, the title again matched the real situation. And all the shoguns from then on were members of the Tokugawa family.

Ieyasu paid due respect to the ancient tradition that the

emperor was the divine ruler of Japan. The emperor concerned himself with matters of religion, learning, and ceremony, assisted by a group of nobles with exalted titles. Ieyasu
left that court structure intact, in Kyoto, and even increased
the funds allotted for its support. Ieyasu also allowed the
daimyo who submitted to him to keep their titles as rulers of
their domains. But he set up his own structure of councils and
officials that in fact governed the nation. This structure soon
developed into a strong bureaucracy that continued to rule,
no matter who was emperor or who was shogun. To ensure a
smooth transition, Ieyasu himself handed the title of shogun
over to one of his sons in 1605, two years after he had received
it, and ruled until his death in 1616 as an "adviser." His advice, of course, no one dared ignore.

Ieyasu located his center of government in the rich plain
around the present city of Tokyo—the plain he had received
from Hideyoshi as a reward for helping to conquer it. He built
a huge castle at the little port of Edo and began to develop the
port into a great city. He had an enormous income from the
lands and cities under his direct rule, but his plans required
even larger sums. He confiscated a gold mine and two silver
mines, and piled up by the time of his death the equivalent of
tons of gold. More than half of this accumulation he be-
queathed to the government treasury. He minted coins that
merchants all over the country could trust as genuine. His
strong government meant that goods could be transported
safely all over Japan, and merchants began trading on a national scale. But their activities were closely supervised by the
government.

Ieyasu continued the policy of requiring the daimyo to
send hostages as pledges of their good behavior, and encouraged the daimyo themselves to live in Edo for some
months every other year. The cost of maintaining a residence
in Edo, and of traveling to and from their home provinces
with hundreds of soldiers and retainers, was a tremendous
drain on the finances of the daimyo, which was exactly what
Ieyasu intended. He wanted them to have neither time nor

money to plot a revolt against him. He also established a nationwide secret police network that reported to him most efficiently every development that might threaten his plan for a stable, long-lasting government. His policies were carried out by the samurai, with their traditional unquestioning loyalty and obedience. He gave Japan a form of government that lasted until 1868—a remarkable stability, achieved at a great cost in terms of freedom and in the ability to develop new ideas.

Ieyasu knew that the village of Nagasaki on the island of Kyushu had developed into a great port in a short time because the European ships stopped there—especially the Portuguese great ships that brought goods from China. He resolved to encourage the European ships to come to Edo. More than that, he resolved to build Japanese ships as big and powerful as the European ones. A tremendous storm at sea delivered to him a remarkable sailor who helped him in both resolves.

The sailor's name was Will Adams. He was born in England in 1568. When he was twelve, he went to London— the London of Queen Elizabeth I, and William Shakespeare. Will Adams signed up as apprentice to a ship builder. By the time he was thirty, he had learned a lot about ships, and also about navigating them. And he had heard a lot of sailors' stories about the "riches of the Orient." He knew the Portuguese and the Spanish had sent ships there by way of the tip of Africa, and Ferdinand Magellan had reached the Orient by sailing around the tip of South America. Portugal and Spain had a near monopoly on trade with the East. But the year Will arrived in London, 1580, an Englishman, Sir Francis Drake, completed a voyage around the world. In 1588, the English defeated the Spanish Armada. In 1597, a Dutchman, Cornelius Houtman, returned from the Orient with a treaty for trade with Java. English and Dutch merchants were determined to challenge the Portuguese and Spanish monopoly.

In 1598, Will Adams signed on as pilot of the ship *Liefde,* one of five Dutch ships that intended to sail together around South America to the Orient. The other four ships were lost at sea. The *Liefde,* her captain dead and her original crew of one hundred and ten reduced to twenty-four, was driven by a storm onto the island of Kyushu, on April 19, 1600. That was six months before Ieyasu won the battle of Sekigahara that made him undisputed ruler of Japan. Ieyasu was very much interested by the news of the arrival of a large European ship with a crew neither Portuguese or Spanish, but Dutch with a few Englishmen. He ordered that the English pilot and a Dutch officer be brought to him.

A Portuguese Jesuit priest served as interpreter at the first meeting between Adams and Ieyasu. In the Jesuit view, Protestant England was a nation of heretics, and the interpreter denounced Adams as a heretic. English buccaneers had been attacking and plundering Portuguese and Spanish ships on the trade routes, so he added that Adams was also probably a pirate. But Ieyasu was principally interested in the nautical charts and the ship's compass Adams had with him, and in his ship. Also, he was an excellent judge of men, and although he understood not a word Adams said, he saw the strength of the man and made him welcome.

The thought of an Englishman having the ear of the powerful Ieyasu pleased the Jesuits not at all. Privately, after the interview was over, they offered to help Adams escape from Japan. But Adams soon concluded that he was safer as a guest of Ieyasu than he would be in the hands of the Jesuits, and he returned to the *Liefde.* Ieyasu ordered that he be given help with repairs to make the ship seaworthy again. Then he ordered Adams to sail it from Kyushu to the developing port of Edo. Adams used the time while the repairs were being made to learn to speak enough Japanese to be able to communicate directly, without the distortions of hostile interpreters. And by the time the *Liefde* reached Edo, Ieyasu was master of the nation.

In Edo, Ieyasu sent Adams to live in the house of an old

soldier, who had two daughters whose company the Englishman found most agreeable. Ieyasu then announced that he
would like to buy the *Liefde* and its guns. Furthermore, he
would like Adams to help him build similar ships so that
Japan would not have to depend on the merchants of other
nations for its trade. By this time the two men had developed
considerable mutual respect. Adams knew there was no hope
he could return to England without Ieyasu's help. He had
been treated well in Japan, for the most part. After due consideration, he replied that he would help build ships, if
Ieyasu would grant him the rank of samurai. Ieyasu agreed.
Adams then asked to be allowed to marry the younger of the
two daughters of the old soldier. Ieyasu agreed again and also
gave Adams a piece of property for their home and a com-
fortable income.

Under Adams's direction, the Japanese built first a ship
of eighty-two tons, somewhat smaller than the *Liefde*, and
then one of one hundred and twenty tons. Japanese trading
voyages increased. Adams became the chief naval adviser in
the government, having earned Ieyasu's complete confidence.
He explained that while the Portuguese and the Spanish came
to Japan with a double objective of teaching their religion
and making a profit from trade, the English and the Dutch
were interested only in trade. That pleased Ieyasu very much,
for like Hideyoshi, he was never free of suspicion that the
Christians, who had won several daimyo to their religion,
were seeking political power.

In 1609, a Dutch trading mission succeeded in reaching
Japan, after a safer voyage than that of the *Liefde*, and established trade relations at the port of Hirado, on a small

*Trade with the West flourished under Ieyasu's rule. This Japanese
painting shows European merchants in Kyoto, the imperial capital. But
Ieyasu's successors feared foreign domination of Japan and forbade all trade
and travel outside the country.*

island northwest of Nagasaki. Ieyasu wanted Europeans to come to his city of Edo. Adams had learned that the London East India Company, formed in 1600, was also planning to send ships to Japan. He wrote advising them to come directly to Edo, rather than stopping in Kyushu where the Dutch were. Sir John Saris, the captain of the first English ship to arrive, either did not see the letter, or chose to ignore the advice of a mere ship's pilot, and went to Hirado. The daimyo there said Sir John must wait until the shogun's naval adviser could be sent for, an Englishman like himself. The wait annoyed Saris no little bit. After Adams interviewed the captain, he took him on the long journey to see Ieyasu. The shogun said he would allow the English to trade anywhere in Japan and would allow them to build a trading station in Edo. Adams urged Saris to accept this offer, but the captain insisted on trading at Hirado. After this inauspicious start, it is not surprising that the English trade did not flourish; it lasted only ten years.

Despite the strained relations between the English samurai Adams and the English knight Saris, the arrival of the ship did set Adams to thinking about home. He was now forty-five years old and had been away for fifteen years. He asked Ieyasu for permission to return to England with the ship, and Ieyasu reluctantly granted it. But in the end, Adams's ties to Japan were too strong to break, and he decided to stay on to help develop the English trade. He died in Japan in 1620.

The activities of the Christians in Japan vexed Ieyasu during all his rule. The Jesuits were continually making accusations about the Franciscans, and vice versa. Then when the Dutch arrived, the Franciscans asked him to expel them from the country. Ieyasu ignored this attempt to tell him how to run his country, and the Franciscans repeated the request, with the insulting addition that Spain would be happy to send her ships to Japanese waters to destroy the Dutch. Ieyasu was a calm and patient man, who rarely let his anger control his actions. He knew that his predecessors had tolerated the Christian priests because of their influence with the European merchants, and he hoped that rivalry between England and Holland and Spain and Portugal would increase trade overall. Since the foreign traders wouldn't come to Edo, he restricted trade to Hirado and Nagasaki, to make it easier to supervise their activities.

In 1613, however, the Christians took actions that Ieyasu could not overlook.

The son of Hideyoshi, five years old at the time of his father's death, was now twenty. Ieyasu had allowed him to live in the castle at Osaka built by Hideyoshi, a formidable fortress. A group of daimyo now sought to overthrow Ieyasu, saying Hideyoshi's son was the rightful ruler of Japan. Among them were several of the daimyo who had been converted to Christianity. This coalition made its headquarters in Osaka Castle. It took Ieyasu two years of hard fighting to overthrow that stronghold. The Christians frequently displayed banners marked with the cross of their religion. And when the castle finally fell, the victors found a number of Jesuits inside its walls.

Also in 1613, twenty-seven Japanese Christians deliberately defied a prohibition against celebrating mass in Edo. They were executed. Their mentor, a Spanish priest, was also sentenced to death, but the sentence was not carried out. In 1614, an edict was issued calling for the expulsion of all foreign priests from Japan. At that time they numbered about one hundred and fifty. Many went into hiding. Some boarded ships leaving Japan, but once the ships were out of sight of land, transferred into small boats and returned to their work. A total of forty-seven escaped expulsion in these ways. Ieyasu was occupied by the struggle for Osaka Castle and took no action against them. His successors would be less tolerant.

In June, 1615, Osaka Castle finally fell. To the Japanese who had threatened his government, Ieyasu showed no

mercy. Thousands were executed. Hideyoshi's son also had
to die, lest other rebels rally around him. Ieyasu allowed him
to commit suicide.

A year later, Ieyasu died, at the age of seventy-four. There
was no problem of succession this time, for his son was already
shogun. After a lengthy period of mourning, Ieyasu was en-
tombed in a magnificent resting place he had prepared ninety
miles north of Edo, at a mountain village, Nikko. Other
shoguns joined him there when they died. Thousands of visitors travel to Nikko every year; it is one of the great pilgrim-
age places of Japan.

Ieyasu's son, whose name was Hidetada, continued his
father's policies and stepped down in favor of his son, Iemitsu. Neither son nor grandson had the confidence born of
many victories that Ieyasu had, nor his great patience. Hidetada renewed the order that the Christian priests leave Japan
and added a new order: all Japanese Christians must renounce their faith, on pain of death. There were about three
hundred thousand Christian Japanese at that time. Many of
these had accepted the religion at the direction of the Christian daimyo and now rejected it with equal ease. But thousands held much deeper religious beliefs and were willing to
die for what they believed. The European priests who were
their spiritual guides seemed almost to ask for martyrdom,
openly defying the shogun's edict. The official responsible for
sending the priests away from Nagasaki decided that he must
make an example, and in 1617, he had two of them decapi-
tated. He had failed to understand the power that martyrs
have in the Christian religion. Great crowds visited the grave
of the two priests. New converts were made. And when the
news reached Portugal, a plan was formed to aid the Japanese
Christians in a new revolt. The shogun learned of this plan
and intensified his efforts to eliminate what he saw as a threat
of a European invasion of Japan. By 1623, when Hidetada
retired, a total of sixteen Jesuit priests had been executed.

The third shogun of the Tokugawa family, Iemitsu, took

even stronger measures to prevent the feared invasion. He allowed all sorts of tortures to be used to persuade Japanese Christians to recant, and in 1623, five hundred who refused were executed. But the European priests kept coming to Japan, and they kept making converts. Finally, Iemitsu made a decision that profoundly affected Japanese history for two hundred years. He decided the only way to keep the priests out was to keep out the merchant ships that brought them. He decreed that the only ships that could visit Japan were those belonging to China and Holland. The Dutch had shown no interest in teaching religion so far, but to be doubly safe, he limited their activities to a small island in Nagasaki harbor. Furthermore, he put an end to foreign voyages by Japanese, the voyages his grandfather Ieyasu had gone to such pains to encourage, and he forbade those Japanese then living abroad to return home, lest they bring some foreign influences with them. These measures, known as the Exclusion Acts, closed the gates of Japan to the western world for two centuries.

The final acts of Christian defiance took place on the peninsula of Shimabara, on the western side of Nagasaki Bay. The region around Nagasaki was the region where the missionaries had had their greatest success, and many of the peasants living there were Christian. But Christian or not, all the peasants suffered from the unusually oppressive rule of the local lords. In 1637, they revolted. Some Christian samurai joined them, and on January 27, 1638, the whole group of rebels, with their wives and children, seized and occupied a castle on the Shimabara peninsula. Their numbers are estimated variously between twenty thousand and thirty-seven thousand people. The Christians among them carried flags and crosses and shouted in battle such cries as "Jesus" and "Maria." It is not surprising that the government viewed the Shimabara Revolt as a religious uprising. After repeated attacks, on April 12, 1638, government forces entered the castle and killed all but a hundred of the people inside. That slaughter put an end to open Christian worship in Japan. But two centuries later, when Christian missionaries were once again allowed in Japan, they found that some few families were still Christians, having transmitted their beliefs secretly from generation to generation.

Outside influences in Japan were now reduced to the lowest level in centuries. Buddhist temples no longer possessed armies and vast lands. Christianity, after ninety years of growth, was effectively suppressed. Foreign trade was greatly reduced. Yet isolation did not result in the stagnation one might expect.

4

A Closed World

 The policy of excluding foreign influence from Japan, instituted by the shoguns early in the seventeenth century, continued for more than two hundred years. During that time Japan developed into a nation with its own special characteristics—a nation unlike any other in the world.

The most important factor contributing to national development was the peace that prevailed almost unbroken in this long period of time. No longer were farmers taken away from the farms to fight to satisfy the ambitions of the daimyo, for all the daimyo were now under the control of the national government. Taxes were high, but they were a known quantity, since extra taxes to pay for wars were no longer levied. With hard work and good planning, a farm family could be assured of enough rice to eat. If the weather was favorable, and no flood or calamity interfered, a family might even have at the end of the year some rice left over.

For centuries, rice, the staple food of the nation, had been

49

the measure of wealth in Japan. The title "daimyo" was earned by gaining control of enough land to produce a certain quantity of rice. Taxes were assessed on the basis of estimated rice production of each piece of land. The wages of the samurai were stated in terms of quantities of rice. Thus rice was the medium of exchange, the money, of feudal Japan.

That system worked well enough when a daimyo lived in his castle in the middle of his lands. The farmers could bring to the castle town the daimyo's share of the rice they grew. His officials could measure the rice out to the samurai in his army. The domain of each daimyo had its own self-sufficient economy. But when Ieyasu brought all sixty-six provinces of Japan under one national government, a national economy became possible. The shogun's government minted coins of gold and silver, which were recognized throughout the nation as worth a certain amount of rice. A dependable system of money backed by the government gave a great boost to national development—and in time led to a great problem.

Now a farm family with rice to spare could sell it. A really determined family could in time earn enough extra to buy additional land to grow more rice, or to grow crops like tobacco or cotton, "cash crops," intended expressly for sale. Less determined families still had a bit extra to buy things to add enjoyment to life, such as tobacco, or the wine called sake made from rice, or good-looking clothes to wear on holidays.

Now a samurai could receive his wages in coins rather than in rice and buy what suited his fancy. A daimyo could use coins to pay the expenses of the regular trips to Edo that were required to show his respect for the shogun. The trouble was, there were rarely enough coins in the purse to pay for all the things a samurai or daimyo wanted. Many found they could still buy, by promising to pay out of next year's wages or next year's taxes. They soon lost track of how much they had promised to pay. The unpaid debts of samurai and daimyo became a serious problem for the shogun's government in the eighteenth century. But in the seventeenth century the new economy based on buying and selling was too enjoyable—and profitable, for some—for gloomy thoughts about debt.

Buying and selling was of course the work of merchants. As mentioned earlier, traditionally, there were four classes in Japan below the nobility: samurai, farmers, craftsmen, merchants. The merchants were considered the lowest of the four. But when peace provided the conditions for national development, it was the merchants who provided the major driving force that pushed development on its way. As their wealth and power increased, the roles of the other classes had to change. John Whitney Hall cites the history of two of the greatest corporations as examples: Mitsui and Sumitomo.

In the 1620s, the Mitsui family brewed sake near the shrine at Ise, sacred to the divine ancestress of the Japanese nation, a shrine much visited by pilgrims, who were thirsty after their long journeys. In 1673, the family had enough money to open a shop in the capital city, Edo, to sell cotton cloth. The shop had several policies unusual in its day. Prices were fixed, not subject to bargaining. Advertising publicized the shop widely. Customers with little to spend were welcomed, since the family preferred many small sales for cash to a few large sales on credit—the wealthy were often slow to pay their bills. In all these ways the shop resembled the modern department store—indeed, the Mitsui company operates department stores all over Japan today under the name Mitsukoshi. Business was brisk, and the family opened shops in Kyoto and Osaka in the 1680s. By the 1690s, the family's financial know-how had won for the Mitsui company appointments as financial agent for the shogun, the emperor, and several daimyo. And its wealth was sufficient for it to finance the draining of some marshland for agriculture, land whose production was added to the family fortunes. Wealth continued to grow, until in the first half of the twentieth century Mitsui was, in Edwin Reischauer's words, "the largest private economic empire in the world."

At the beginning of the seventeenth century, the Sumitomo family of Kyoto sold wares made of iron. Then they began to trade in a more valuable metal, copper, shipped through the growing port of Osaka. They set up their own copper refineries in both Kyoto and Osaka. They too became agents for the government, and in 1791, began to develop new copper mines to supply the demand. Today the great Sumitomo Steel Works are a major factor in world steel production.

As these two examples show, the simple desire to make a profit in trade, coupled with sound business sense, led to the development of new farms and mines that increased the total real wealth of the nation. Most important, a close relationship between businessmen and the government developed that has continued. This relationship has been a major factor in the nation's rise to the status of a world power.

The last years of the seventeenth century are called in Japan the Era of Prosperity. Many people had the leisure to enjoy the arts, which developed rapidly in this period. City dwellers enjoyed two new forms of theatrical entertainment. First there was the puppet theater, where puppets two-thirds life size acted out stories of famous samurai, or of young lovers separated by the demands of family or country. Soon, in the kabuki theater, similar stories were being acted out by flesh and blood actors. With brilliant staging, extravagant costumes, and careful attention to the interpretation of character, kabuki developed into one of the world's greatest theatrical forms. The dramatist Chikamatsu Monzaemon wrote plays on a wide variety of subjects for both the puppet and kabuki stages. The classic dramas of Japan, called the

The Kabuki theater, with its exciting plots and elaborate costumes, was one of the favorite pastimes in the Era of Prosperity of the late seventeenth century.

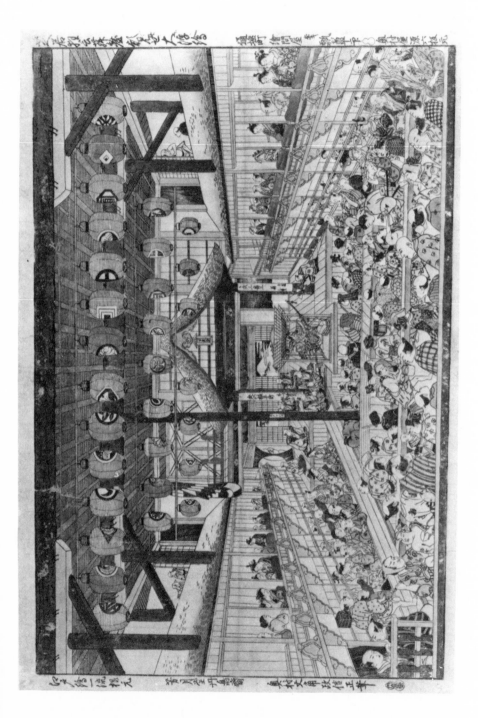

noh plays, continued to be performed also. Many novels were printed to satisfy the national love of a good story.

Much attention was paid to music, with the three-stringed instrument, the samisen, especially popular. Poetry, always enjoyed by the upper classes in Japan, reached a wider audience with the development of the short poem known as the haiku: a line of five syllables, followed by a line of seven syllables, ending with another line of five. The master of the haiku was Matsuo Munefusa, who wrote using the penname Basho. He created word pictures of objects in nature to give insights into the meaning of life.

Talented women gave years of study to learning the arts of music and literature in order to become geisha, professional entertainers highly respected for their skills. A woman who was accomplished enough was employed in a geisha house, where she would sing, play the samisen, recite poetry and chat with a patron. Sometimes her most important service was to provide a sympathetic ear as a man told her his troubles. Her role was often misunderstood by westerners, who confused the geisha with the prostitute, a professional class whose services were also widely available in Japanese cities.

Theaters, geisha houses, sake shops and teahouses tended to cluster together in urban districts called "nightless cities," where sleep seemed unknown. Entertainment was the primary goal. The Japanese called the men and women who provided the entertainment the "floating world" (ukiyo).

To make opportunities for pleasure known to prospective customers, the entrepreneurs of the floating world needed to advertise. As a result, the period saw a marvelous development of the art of the wood-block print. The Japanese soon recognized that the best of these wood-block prints had a beauty that overshadowed the simple advertising message they delivered. Prints came to be valued for themselves, as works of art. Some print makers turned to subjects beyond the world of entertainment—landscapes were particularly favored. The prints were produced in great numbers and sold cheaply.

Matsuo Munefusa, called Basho, was born in 1644 into a samurai family, but he chose to write instead of fight. He became one of the great masters of the seventeen-syllable Japanese poem, the haiku.

This art was practiced most notably by Moronobu, who died in 1714, and in the next two centuries by Utamaro, Hokusai and Hiroshige. Because of its origin, the name "floating world" has become attached to the Japanese wood-block print. In the nineteenth century the work of the Japanese masters was much admired in Europe. They had a strong influence on Henri Toulouse-Lautrec, for example, who made color lithographs to advertise the entertainment opportunities of the City of Light, Paris.

Clearly the merchants were not suffering too much from their position as the lowest class in society. They probably enjoyed the Era of Prosperity more than any other class. And if they wanted to, they could sometimes find a way into another class. A wealthy man could pay to be "adopted" into the family of a samurai who needed cash. A beautiful girl had an appeal that crossed all class lines. A notable example was the mother of the shogun who ruled throughout the Era of Prosperity. She was the daughter of a grocer in Kyoto.

Keishoin is the name this remarkable woman is remembered by. She was born in 1625. Her father supplied food to various important families in Kyoto. Her mother worked as a servant for one of these families. As an attractive girl in her teens, she was noticed by that family, and by their relatives who visited them. One relative decided she would help the girl and took her to Edo, to the palace of the third Tokugawa shogun, Iemitsu. Soon Iemitsu noticed her too, and when she was twenty years old she bore him a son. When this son was thirty-five, he was named the fifth Tokugawa shogun, Tsunayoshi. Keishoin had a strong, if not always beneficial, influence on his policies.

The strong bureaucracy established by Tsunayoshi's great-grandfather Ieyasu was governing Japan very successfully. Tsunayoshi was content that it continue to do so, while he gave his attention to religion, philosophy, and art. He loved the theater, and acted roles in noh plays himself. But the actions for which he is most remembered were the result of Keishoin's firm belief in the teachings of Buddhism.

Since the Buddhists believe in reincarnation, the return

of the spirit after death in another body, they have a responsibility to protect all living things. Tsunayoshi had no male heir. His mother and he became convinced that this was a punishment because in an earlier incarnation he had taken the life of some creature, and that the remedy was to work vigorously to protect life now. Since the year of his birth was, by the Buddhist calendar, the Year of the Dog, he became especially zealous for the welfare of Edo's large population of dogs. Tsunayoshi's mind became quite unbalanced on the subject, and edicts poured forth. Dogs should not be harmed. Dogs should be spoken to with respect, as Mr. Dog or Mrs. Dog. Soon Edo's streets were so filled with dogs that the city had to gather them up and care for them in special shelters. It was reported that at one time fifty thousand dogs were being fed rice and fish, bought with tax money. Not surprisingly, Tsunayoshi is sometimes known as "the dog shogun."

He deserves a better title than that, for it was during the twenty-nine years he ruled (1680–1709) that a major national problem was largely solved: the problem of finding suitable occupations for a large group of proud warriors, the samurai, in an era of peace. In 1592, Hideyoshi had sent them to invade Korea with disastrous results. Now a better solution came from the philosophic studies Tsunayoshi loved and encouraged.

The samurai principles of loyalty, simple living, and passionate protection of honor had developed in times of war. They served the needs of the nation and of the individual samurai, then. But now in the Tokugawa shoguns' long reign of peace, the samurai were as restless as professional athletes between seasons. Some of them left the castle towns of the daimyo and went roaming about the countryside looking for something to do. They were known as *ronin*, "masterless samurai." Some took up a craft. Most simply collected their pay from the daimyo and sat around the castle towns, bored, complaining that their money bought less and less because prices were going up.

The daimyo were required by the shogun not only to pay the samurai for doing nothing, but also to look after all sorts of local matters necessary to governing the country: taxes, roads, law courts, regulation of commerce, and so on. The cities were growing, the national economy was growing, the government was becoming more complex. The daimyo had very few people with enough education to cope with such matters. A samurai who turned up his nose at learning addition and subtraction—"merchant skills"—would not be much help with taxes, however. And one accustomed to dealing out instant justice with his sword would not have the patience for the slow procedures of a law court.

A solution was suggested repeatedly by scholars over a period of years. It was really put into practice under Tsunayoshi, a shogun who was something of a scholar himself. The suggestion came from the scholars' study of the country the Japanese most admired, China.

The samurai were the highest class of the four classes traditionally recognized in Japan, above the farmers, craftsmen and merchants, and just below the nobility. In the West we have a phrase, "an officer and a gentleman," that gives an idea of the way these elite Japanese warriors viewed themselves. But in China, military prowess was much less esteemed. There the class just below the nobility was made up of men of learning. We have another phrase, "a gentleman and a scholar," that can be applied to them. A three-part man, "an officer and a gentleman and a scholar," seems unheard of in East or West, except for a few rare individuals. But that was the ideal the Japanese scholars set before the samurai in the seventeenth century. They should be leaders in times of peace as well as in times of war. The way to achieve that was to balance military training with study of philosophy. From study, they would learn how to issue wise orders that the people would gladly obey, and how to live such good lives that the people would gladly follow their examples. This was all in keeping with the teaching of the greatest Chinese sage, Confucius, that good government is possible only when the ruler is himself good and maintains a good relationship with his loyal subjects.

That ideal was never achieved in Japan (and rarely in China) but it did lead some of the samurai to study at schools established around the nation by various daimyo and by the shogun. Tsunayoshi founded the greatest of these, in Edo, and undoubtedly his genuine interest in learning did serve as an example to the samurai. "The samurai are losing their military spirit," some people complained, and indeed they were. But the nation needed government officials, and by the end of Tsunayoshi's rule, the class of warriors had been largely transformed into a class of bureaucrats.

Perhaps the clearest example of the blending of samurai skills with philosophy can be seen in the development that took place about this time in the martial arts: kendo, judo and karate. The training that had made the samurai such formidable opponents on the battlefield was now adapted to sports competitions that kept body and mind in peak condition. Kendo, Japanese fencing, was a peaceful equivalent of swordsmanship. Judo, or jujitsu, had begun as a method of self-defense in the event a warrior had his sword taken from him. Karate, imported into Japan from Okinawa around 1610, had a similar purpose; the karate expert uses his bare hands instead of any weapon. (The literal meaning of the word is "empty hand.") Success in all three of these martial arts depended on concentration, attitude, spiritual preparation— Western athletes speak of "psyching up" for a contest, but it goes deeper than that for the Japanese. There was time to develop and enjoy all these sports during the Tokugawa peace. There was also time for that great sport of Japan enjoyed on a simpler level, sumo (Japanese professional wrestling).

In 1702, the changed status of the samurai was made very clear in a punishment given by the shogun's government to a group of forty-seven *ronin*, masterless samurai. The Case of the Forty-Seven Ronin was high drama in real life, and it has been a favorite subject of Japanese playwrights ever since. At issue was the government's responsibility for maintaining law and order, versus the samurai principle: "A man must not live under the same sky as one who has injured his lord or his father."

One day, in the shogun's castle, a lord named Kira insulted another lord, named Asano. Greatly offended, Asano drew his sword and wounded Kira before the two could be separated. Violence in the castle was strictly prohibited, and Asano was condemned to commit *seppuku*, ritual suicide, which he did.

Kira's insult had thus caused the death of Asano, leaving his forty-seven loyal samurai without a master. They resolved to avenge Asano, at any cost. Their leader knew Kira would expect that. To get him to relax his guard, the samurai leader pretended to drown his sorrow in alcohol, and for many months gave the appearance of a man who had lost all purpose in life. Then one snowy morning the forty-seven ronin met, forced their way into Kira's house, cut off his head and carried it to their dead master's grave. Then they surrendered themselves to the government. Ordinary people in Japan viewed the forty-seven as noble heroes, and even many members of the government were reluctant to see them punished. But at last the decision was reached that they should join their master in death. They committed seppuku and were buried beside him. It was a clear signal that all Japanese must be ruled by the shogun's government.

The government of the Tokugawa shoguns lasted for another century and a half, to 1868—a total of 265 years. Ten more members of the Tokugawa family were named shogun, after Tsunayoshi. Some were wise and strong, and some were not. Ieyasu, the first Tokugawa shogun, had planned the structure of the government so that it would endure, no matter who was shogun. It finally ended not because of failure but because of success: Japan under the Tokugawas flourished to such an extent that it outgrew the structure.

The population grew. It rose from about twenty million in 1600 to thirty million in 1721. Edo, a village when Ieyasu made it his capital, was a city of more than half a million in 1721—larger than Kyoto, and as large as any city in the world at that time. The national wealth grew. Some merchant families had fortunes that equaled the wealth of some daimyo. And the bureaucracy grew. As the nation grew, there was more work for the bureaucracy to do, so some growth was necessary. But as much as seven percent of the total population of Japan belonged to samurai families, and the sons of samurai followed their fathers into government. Often useless posts were created for them to fill. In time the grandsons of the samurai who had been paid to sit around barracks and do nothing were paid to sit around government offices and do nothing. And like their grandfathers, they complained that their wages would not buy as much because prices were going up. Worse than the wastefulness of overstaffed offices was the problem of too much dependence on "what grandfather would have done" in a given situation. New situations were arising, and the hereditary bureaucracy was ill-suited to deal with change.

One part of Japan lagged behind the others in growth: its agriculture. The peasants, traditionally second only to samurai in the ranking of classes, faced natural limits on how much they could increase the crops they grew. Japan is a very mountainous country, with much of its area impossible for farming. Some years bad weather ruined the crops or swarms of insects ate them up. In such years the government supplied rice from its storehouses to keep the peasants from starvation. Farm production grew, but not at the same rate as other sections of the economy. And the peasants could achieve nothing like the wealth of the merchants, no matter how hard they worked. The gap between the two groups caused resentment, and sometimes riots.

By about 1700, the population had reached the maximum that could be fed by Japanese agriculture, so population growth slowed and almost stopped in the eighteenth century. Other countries as rich as Japan would have bought food from neighboring nations, but the shogun's policy of exclusion forbade that for Japan.

There was also a maximum for the number of samurai bureaucrats the shogun's government and the daimyo could support. The complaint that pay did not keep pace with rising prices was accurate. But in order to raise the pay of the samurai, many daimyo had to borrow money from the rich merchants. If the daimyo did not raise pay, the samurai had to borrow money from the merchants. So great debts piled up in the eighteenth century. Even the shogun's government, so wealthy in the time of Ieyasu, was running low on funds. Most of the shoguns after Tsunayoshi were content to leave the increasingly complex affairs of government to high-ranking counselors, who dealt with them with varying degrees of competence and honesty.

One shogun in the eighteenth century did work very hard at governing the country: Yoshimune, the eighth Tokugawa shogun, who ruled from 1716 to 1745. He recognized the problems of the peasants, the samurai, and the daimyo and took some sensible steps to deal with them. A major expense of every daimyo was the journey to Edo he was required to make every other year with a great retinue. This requirement had been instituted expressly to prevent any daimyo from becoming rich enough to challenge the shogun's rule. Now, after a century of peace, Yoshimune allowed the daimyo to "show their loyalty" by less frequent visits. Part of the money they saved, however, he required them to contribute to the government's treasury, to help pay the bureaucrats. He ordered cutbacks in government personnel and decreed that pay levels should be related to merit. He replaced the fixed tax on rice production, which was based on the area of land cultivated, with a tax that varied from year to year as actual production varied. He repealed an edict that forbade the people to appeal directly to the shogun for help and ordered that every appeal be evaluated. He limited use of torture in the questioning of suspected criminals and reduced the very severe punishments customary for relatively minor offenses.

These measures were helpful, at least for a time. Yoshimune also issued some orders that showed that he, like many another ruler, overrated his power. He ordered the people to live more frugally—especially the samurai and the daimyo. Some of these orders were quite specific: "Women's dress has of recent years become more and more showy. Hereafter even the wives of daimyo shall not use more than a small amount of gold-thread embroidery in their garments and shall not wear dresses made of costly fabric." None of these orders were obeyed. To combat inflation, which was so painful to samurai living on fixed incomes, he tried to control the price of rice, which helped some people and harmed others in ways he had not intended.

But Yoshimune understood that he must also seek long-range solutions to Japan's problems. Food was the most pressing one. He instituted a program to reclaim land from marshes, to increase rice production. And he sought a crop that would be an alternative to rice. His final choice was the sweet potato, which a scholar reported was grown in the Ryukyu Islands south of Japan. Yoshimune was curious about other lands, like the first Tokugawa shogun, Ieyasu, whom he admired very much. He decided to allow books from China to be imported again, provided they contained no Christian teachings—the dangerous teachings that had so frightened Ieyasu's timid successors. And he also commissioned scholars to study Western science, especially medicine, astronomy, and military tactics. Since the only Westerners allowed in Japan for the past hundred years were the Dutch traders on their little island in the harbor of Nagasaki, he directed scholars to learn the Dutch language. Western knowledge in Japan was long called "Dutch learning." From the time of Yoshimune, there was a slowly growing awareness of the great progress being made in Europe

An eighteenth-century woodblock print shows Japanese ladies in luxurious kimono enjoying a picnic. The eighth shogun of the Tokugawa family, Yoshimune (ruled 1716-1745), urged a return to the virtues of frugality and hard work, but few among the wealthy listened.

and in a new land called America in the period we call the Industrial Revolution.

At about the same time, some scholars reexamined the long-held idea that China was the country deserving to be most admired and imitated by Japan. Undoubtedly there was much to be learned from Chinese culture, especially the teachings of Confucius. But Japan was a small nation of islands, while China was a vast nation on the mainland of Asia. Perhaps some adaptation was necessary, the scholars felt. Such thoughts led to renewed study of Japan's history. And study of history, pursued back to the nation's beginnings, merged with the study of the Shinto religion. For Shinto taught that the islands and people of Japan were created by two deities, whose great-great-great-great grandson was the first emperor of Japan. His descendants had ruled as emperors in an unbroken line—by far the longest rule by one family of any nation.

Large numbers of Japanese drew two related conclusions from such studies of history and religion. First, Japan was something special among nations, very likely better than other nations. Second, the difficulties the government was having might be attributed to the fact that the emperor was never consulted on questions of policy; he performed only ceremonial functions. A few men even suggested that the shogun's government might well be replaced by a new government directed by the emperor. But as long as the bureaucracy was providing stable rule and relative prosperity for most of the people, there was little pressure for change. Emperor succeeded emperor and shogun succeeded shogun in an orderly fashion, unaffected in any practical way by the questions of the philosophers and historians.

Then, as the eighteenth century ended, some new questions reached the shogun and emperor. This time the questioners were not Japanese, but Russians, Englishmen, and Americans.

5
The Gates
Forced Open

 A look at a world globe shows that the continents of North America and Asia very nearly meet in the areas now known as the state of Alaska and the Soviet Republic of Yakutsk in Siberia. Running southwest from the meeting place is a string of islands, roughly parallel to the coast of Asia. From north to south they are the Aleutian Islands, the Kurile Islands, the Japanese Islands, the Ryukyu Islands, and the Philippine Islands. In the sixteenth and seventeenth centuries, three great sea powers, Portugal, Spain, and Holland, had established trading relations with Japan. The Japanese called the people of these nations "the Southern Barbarians," because they always approached Japan from the south—the Portuguese and Dutch having sailed around the tip of Africa, and the Spanish having sailed across the Pacific from their colony in Mexico.

In the eighteenth and nineteenth centuries, three additional nations sought trade with Japan: Russia, England, and the United States of America. But by this time, Japan had adopted its Exclusion Policy, forbidding all foreign trade except the trade with the Dutch merchants living in Nagasaki. Changing this policy was no easy matter.

The first to make the attempt were the Russians. At the beginning of the eighteenth century, Peter the Great, one of the most forceful rulers Russia ever had, was determined to develop the vast region of Siberia. (The government of the Soviet Union today has a similar goal.) Siberia is rich in natural resources, but it is terribly inaccessible. Land transport in Peter's day was limited to what pack animals could carry on their backs. The sea route from the port of St. Petersburg on the Baltic Sea to Okhotsk in Siberia took a year or more. Furthermore, the harbors of Siberia, clogged with ice ten months in the year, were open only in August and September. But ships were the only way to carry heavy cargoes from Siberia's mines and forests.

The chances of success of any voyage were greatly improved if a ship could stop at friendly ports along the way to obtain food and water. In the case of a voyage to Siberia, Peter's ships also needed a place to wait for the ice to melt. A port in Japan would be ideal. With characteristic vigor, Peter ordered that Dutch books on the Japanese language be studied by linguists in Moscow, and sent ships to explore the Kurile Islands, which lie between Russia and Japan. Peter died before these efforts produced any official contacts between the two countries, but the voyages of exploration continued.

Toward the end of the eighteenth century, Russia had another forceful ruler, Catherine the Great. She renewed efforts to establish official relations with Japan, and in 1792, her envoy arrived at the port of Nemuro on the north island, Hokkaido. To ensure a favorable reception, he had with him some Japanese castaways who had been well treated in Russia. He requested permission to travel to Edo to negotiate for trade. His request was refused. In 1804, the Russians sent an ambassador to Nagasaki, but the shogun's government again refused to negotiate. Although both Russian requests were denied, they caused considerable discussion in Edo. Some members of the government felt that the island of Hokkaido, with a sparse population, should be developed as a source of food for the other more densely populated islands of Japan. Trade with the Russians would be a help in such development. The whole Exclusion Policy might have been reexamined, had the Russian ambassador been willing to wait.

All dealings with the shogun's government required great patience. Unfortunately the Russian ambassador did not have that patience. He decided to try to force the Japanese to open trade. With no authorization from anyone, he sent a ship to attack settlements in Hokkaido, in 1807. But this violence caused the shogun's government to resolve to strengthen Japan's defenses to keep foreigners out.

To make matters worse, the next year, 1808, a British warship sailed into Nagasaki harbor and its captain forced the governor of the city to provide it with supplies. Several other British ships forced their way into Japanese ports, and in 1824, there was fighting between some British sailors and some Japanese.

All these incidents combined to cause the shogun's government to issue a new edict in 1825, called the "No Second Thought Expulsion Order." Any foreign vessel that came close to the shores of Japan was to be destroyed, and its crew arrested or killed. Local authorities were directed to take these actions at once, without taking "second thought," and without need for specific authorization from Edo. Previously, ships in genuine need of water and supplies had been allowed brief visits, but now all visits were forbidden. The new edict showed not that the shogun's government was strong, but that it was weak.

In 1840, the British took other actions, which did not involve Japan directly, but were closely watched in Edo. Britain was eager to expand her trade with China. Only one port in China, Canton, was open to foreign merchants, for the same reason that only Nagasaki in Japan was open: to enable the government to control the activities of the merchants more easily.

For some years British merchants had been selling the drug opium, grown in India, to Chinese addicts. The emperor of China ordered that this drug trade be stopped, and his commissioner in the port of Canton seized and burned a large quantity of opium belonging to the British. Britain demanded payment for the opium destroyed and, when the emperor refused, sent warships to enforce the demand. War followed, the "Opium War." The Chinese forces were no match for the British fleet, which captured and held for a time the ports of Canton and Shanghai and the city of Nanking. By the Treaty of Nanking, signed in 1842, Britain got outright possession of the island of Hong Kong, near Canton, and the right to trade in five Chinese ports.

In the Orient, China had long been regarded as the mightiest nation in the world. The news that she had not been able to resist the British fleet caused great consternation in Japan. If China could be forced to yield to British demands, could Japan hope to resist? Some daimyo urged that Japan begin trade with the West at once, in order to buy modern weapons to strengthen her defenses. But the Exclusion Policy had been in effect for two centuries, and to change it seemed to most Japanese an unthinkable violation of law handed down by their ancestors. The shogun's government reaffirmed its policy that trade was forbidden, but that "Western learning" could be pursued so that the Japanese could learn to make modern weapons themselves.

A few of the strongest daimyo began to act on that suggestion. In southern Kyushu, the area where Western muskets had first been introduced in 1543, the daimyo of Satsuma province set about learning to make and use West-

ern artillery the same year the Chinese signed the treaty with
Britain. Later the province recruited samurai for a Western
style navy. Such an effort was costly and possible in only a
few provinces, where the daimyo were not already hopelessly
in debt. Those provinces, however, soon had military forces
that were as strong as the forces of the shogun's government.
And now that the daimyo were required to pay their re-
spects in Edo less often, some of them lost their habit of unquestioning acceptance of policies and edicts of the shogun's
government. All the daimyo agreed that the important thing
was to defend Japan and the emperor from the foreigners.
They would all unite to do that. The disagreements came
over the question of how best to defend their nation.

The third nation that questioned the Exclusion Policy in
the nineteenth century had not even existed when the policy
was adopted. It was a new nation, the United States of
America. In the decade of the 1840s the United States had
developed a great interest in the Pacific Ocean. In 1846, the
British had recognized United States rights to Oregon. In
1848, Spain had turned over her colony of California as a result of the Mexican War. In 1849, the discovery of gold in
California had begun the Gold Rush. There was talk of
building a railroad all the way across the North American
continent, and of opening a regular steamship route across
the Pacific to China. All the major nations of Europe were
intent on developing trade with the Far East, where millions
of people seemed a huge market for their manufactured
goods. The most direct route from Europe to China lay
across North America. And the Americans wanted to have
their share of Far Eastern trade, too. In addition, the waters
of the North Pacific were the home of thousands of whales.
At one time as many as five hundred Yankee whalers were
hunting those waters. For all these reasons, American attention was directed across the Pacific.

Japan lies on the direct route from California to China

and near the best whaling grounds. It didn't make sense to the big-hearted Americans for the Japanese to refuse to sell coal to steamships, or food and water to whaling ships. And if a ship was in distress near Japan, it was downright uncharitable for the Japanese to refuse aid to the crew. Trade would be good for both nations, and clearly Japan could use some good Christian missionaries, too. The problem, as the United States government saw it, was simply how to make the Japanese understand where Japan's best interests lay. Such reasoning was plainly biased by American ambitions, but as events proved, trade was indeed good for both nations. As an aid to understanding, the Americans sent four warships to Edo. Commanding them was the highest ranking officer in the United States Navy, Commodore Matthew Calbraith Perry.

Perry was a member of a family with a distinguished naval tradition. His brother, Oliver Hazard Perry, was the hero of the Battle of Lake Erie in the War of 1812. Matthew Perry himself had commanded in the Mexican War the largest United States naval force ever assembled, in the successful attack on the port of Veracruz. He was experienced in diplomacy, having represented his country in negotiations in Nigeria, Naples, and Canada. He was a strong advocate of giving the navy the advantages of steam to replace sails; two of the warships he sailed into Edo Bay were steam powered. In addition to his experience, Perry had many personal qualities that made him an excellent choice for the mission. He threw himself into every task he undertook with enormous energy and concentration, and his enthusiasm was contagious. He prepared for his visit to Japan by reading everything about the country available in America, and by interviewing everyone he could find who had been there. He was a handsome man, of imposing size and impeccable grooming, fond of inventing little touches of drama to increase the impression he made on those he met. Some called him "vain," but his personality was well suited to dealing with the status-conscious Japanese. Most important of all, he had ample reserves of patience.

In the fall of 1852, Perry sailed from Annapolis for Japan. President Millard Fillmore visited him on board ship to bid farewell. The departure was widely publicized, for Perry wanted the Japanese to know that he was coming, and that his government attached so much importance to his mission that he would not easily be turned away. Actually he was the fourth commodore of the United States Navy sent to Japan since 1845. None of the others had made any progress in opening trade.

On the morning of Friday, July 8, 1853, Perry approached the entrance to Edo Bay on his flagship *Susquehanna*. Here are the words of his own account:

> The steamer, in spite of the wind, moved on with all sails furled, at the rate of eight or nine knots, much to the astonishment of the crews of the Japanese fishing junks . . . who stood up in their boats, and were evidently expressing the liveliest surprise at the sight of the first steamer ever beheld in Japanese waters. As the day advanced the sun came out with a brighter luster. . . . The great Fuji, now, as the fog occasionally lifted, rose to view, and its conelike summit was disclosed, rising to an enormous height. . . . As the ships neared the bay, signals were given by the commodore, and instantly the decks were cleared for action . . . sentinels and men at their posts. . . . When the squadron had approached within two miles of the land a fleet of large boats . . . pushed off with the seeming intention of visiting them. They were, however, not waited for, and were soon left behind, much puzzled, doubtless, by the rapid progress of the steamers against the wind. . . . At about five o'clock in the afternoon the squadron came to anchor off the city of Uraga, on the western side of the bay of Edo.

Perry had no intention of letting his ships be "visited" by crowds of curious Japanese, as other foreign ships had been, in an atmosphere rather like a sideshow at a circus. He was the representative of the president of the United States of America. Any visitors on board must be duly certified representatives of the emperor of Japan. Happily the speed of the steamers was enough to prevent any visits that first day, and there was no need for any warlike action. Had Perry been looking for omens, he would have been greatly encouraged by the fact that Fujiyama, the sacred volcano of Japan, showed itself to him on his arrival. Many visitors spend weeks or months in Japan without having the clouds around the peak lift to reveal that glorious sight.

As Perry had intended, news of his mission had reached Edo some time before his actual arrival. The members of the shogun's government could not agree on what response to make to him, so resolved to delay making any response.

Ordinary citizens were at first frightened and then fascinated by the steamships. News reporters traveled from Edo to Uraga, accompanied by artists who drew hundreds of sketches of the ships and the strange-looking men on board. Japanese ships were made of unpainted wood. These ships were painted, and the color chosen was black. The Japanese customarily referred to them as "the black ships."

Perry now began a carefully considered course of action intended to show the Japanese that they were dealing with a person of great importance. When the vice-governor of Uraga came in a boat to ask Perry what his business was, he got the reply that the commodore would speak only to the representative of the emperor. The vice-governor could speak to a lieutenant. The vice-governor returned to shore, and the governor came out. Perry continued to practice what he called "his own exclusive policy." But his officers, after considerable negotiations, arranged for a prince to come to Uraga to receive from Perry a letter from President Fillmore containing several requests. Perry acknowledged that

On July 14, 1853, Commodore Matthew Perry of the United States Navy (right center) delivered to representatives of the emperor a letter from President Millard Fillmore. It requested that foreign trade, forbidden since the early seventeenth century, be allowed again.

it might take some time for the emperor to decide on his answer to the letter and promised to leave Japan and return after some months for the reply, adding that at that time a larger squadron would accompany him.

Both Japanese and Americans made elaborate preparations for the ceremony of delivering the letter. The Japanese built a colorful pavilion of silk and cotton fabrics of

呈翰握々緋三包
童子二人持之

隊長

惣大将

亞墨利加人久里濱上陸行軍之圖
惣人數五百余人

many colors, decorated with the imperial coat of arms, and
lined up five thousand or more soldiers on the shore, all in
their dress uniforms. Perry took ashore one hundred marines,
one hundred sailors and every officer from the four ships who
was not absolutely required on board. The bands from the two
steamers accompanied them. The letter itself was bound in
blue velvet. Two carefully chosen young men carried it and
Perry's credentials in a procession just to the pavilion. The
commodore walked between two tall blacks, "armed to the
teeth," who served as his personal guard. "All this parade was
but for effect," he reported.

The effect was a good one. The letter was delivered, and Perry was given a paper which read:

The letter of the president of the United States of North America, and copy, are hereby received and will be delivered to the emperor.

It has been many times intimated that business relating to foreign countries cannot be transacted here in Uraga, but at Nagasaki; nevertheless, as it has been observed that the admiral, in his quality of ambassador of the president, would feel himself insulted by a refusal to receive the letter at this place, the justice of which has been acknowledged, the above-mentioned letter is hereby received, in opposition to the Japanese laws.

As this is not the place wherein to negotiate with foreigners, so neither can conferences nor entertainment be held. Therefore, as the letter has been received you can depart.

The words "received in opposition to the Japanese laws" marked Perry's first significant success. Next was the need to persuade the Japanese to grant President Fillmore's requests. They were really quite modest: trade, at least for a short time on a trial basis; humane treatment of American sailors in distress; and the sale of coal for American steamers. The letter was signed "Your good friend, Millard Fillmore."

Despite all the mentions of the emperor, when Perry sailed away with his implied threat of returning with a larger squadron in some months, it was the shogun's government that had to decide what reply to make. And the shogun was no longer powerful enough to take arbitrary action in the name of the entire nation. The shogun's chief adviser asked for the opinions of the daimyo—an unprecedented move, which underlined the weakness of the central government. Two replies favored opening Japan to trade, fourteen favored a course of conciliatory delay, and thirty-four advised rejection of the requests.

Compromise seemed the only possible way to go. The government resolved to grant Perry as little as possible and to do as much as possible to build up military strength before he returned, in case he resorted to force.

On February 11, 1854, Perry returned to Edo Bay with eight ships. The shogun's government sent five commissioners to negotiate with him at the village of Yokohama. They did everything they could to delay granting President Fillmore's requests, but Perry pointed out politely that if he went home without accomplishing the purposes of his mission, his government would probably send an even larger squadron of ships to Japan. He also mentioned that the treaty China had signed with Britain seemed a good model for Japan—an implied threat that the force Britain had used to open Chinese ports might also be applied to Japan.

Finally, on March 31, 1854, the commissioners and Perry signed the Treaty of Kanagawa, which assured American castaways of good treatment in Japan; permitted American ships to obtain supplies at two ports—Shimoda, a hundred miles south of Edo, and Hakodate on the north island of Hokkaido; and authorized the appointment at a later date of a consul to arrange American trade in Japan.

The treaty had to be approved, of course, by the president of the United States and ratified by the Senate and approved by the shogun's government. The Senate ratified it at once. In Japan, approval took much longer. As the government had foreseen, the British, the Dutch, and the Russians immediately requested similar agreements, which the Japanese had no choice but to grant.

In August, 1856, the American consul arrived to take up his post in the port of Shimoda. His name was Townsend Harris. Like Perry, he was both determined and patient. He proceeded to press the Japanese to open ports not just to ships in need of supplies, but to full trade. Harris also asked that Americans be allowed to live in the ports in order to establish regular trading facilities, and that Americans in Japan be granted "extraterritorial status," meaning their conduct

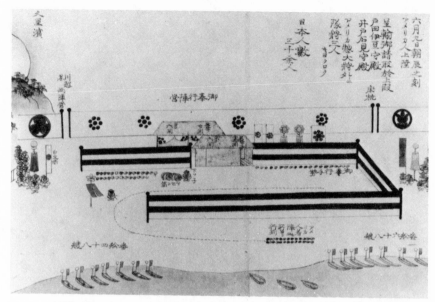

The Japanese received Commodore Perry in a pavilion near the shore thirty miles south of Edo (today's Tokyo). Many banners and brightly colored screens of cloth, bearing the imperial coat of arms, decorated the site.

would be regulated by the laws of their home country rather than by the laws of Japan. After nearly a year and a half of delays, he negotiated a draft of an additional treaty containing these provisions.

In the four years since Perry had first visited Edo Bay, many Japanese had become reconciled to the necessity of admitting foreign trade, but many others opposed the terms of the new treaty. They especially objected to the fact that the treaty did not give to Japan the right to trade in the United States; the treaty was "unequal," or one-sided. All Japanese saw that the inability to resist the foreigners was an indication of how weak the shogun's government had become. Some said it was time to end the two and a half centuries of rule by the Tokugawa shoguns.

In the preceding century, students of history had discussed the idea of giving the emperor a more active part in the government. Now men of action began to discuss that idea. Kyoto became a center of political ferment. A popular slogan was "Honor the emperor, expel the barbarians." Some of the powerful daimyo began to involve the emperor and the nobles of his court in discussions of national policy, for the first time in centuries.

In an effort to silence the opposition to the new treaty, the head of the shogun's government took the unusual step of carrying the treaty to Kyoto to get the emperor's approval for it. In earlier years, such approval would have been assumed. This time the emperor objected. One of the ports to be opened to trade was Osaka, very near to Kyoto. The emperor did not like that. Furthermore, he suggested that the shogun's government should pay more attention to the opinions of the most powerful of the daimyo. And privately, the emperor let it be known that he felt an effort was being made by the shogun's government to coerce him. All this created an uproar.

In August of that same year, 1858, the shogun died: Iesada, the thirteenth Tokugawa shogun. The government's Council of Elders appointed a "Great Councillor" to act almost as a dictator to restore the authority of the central government. The man they chose was strong enough for the task: he selected the next shogun, put under house arrest a daimyo who was leading opposition to the government, and signed the treaty with the United States. The British, Russians and Dutch insisted on, and got, similar treaties, and this time they were joined by the French. But the Great Councillor's actions caused much resentment, which increased when foreigners began to arrive in Japan. In 1860, he was assassinated by a group of samurai retainers of the daimyo he had arrested.

Other samurai burned buildings of the foreigners and even killed a few. In retaliation, warships of several nations bombarded Japanese ports. The shogun's government was less and less able to control the situation. The daimyo of the

In 1854 Commodore Perry returned to Japan and signed a treaty allowing limited trade. He gave the Japanese numerous samples of American products, including a small steam train and two "telegraph instruments" with a mile of wire.

provinces that had acquired Western arms—especially Satsuma in southern Kyushu and Choshu at the western end of the island of Honshu—resolved to take independent action to defend their provinces. Their Western armies were led by capable younger samurai. These samurai, realizing their strength, decided to go even further, to establish a new government under the emperor and abolish the title of shogun.

One of the young samurai directed to study Western military technology became in time the leading statesman of Japan. He was Ito Hirobumi, born in 1841 into a samurai family of Choshu. He saw that the best way to learn about the West was to go there. Under the Exclusion Laws, to leave Japan was an offense punishable by death. Nevertheless Ito and four other young men arranged to be smuggled on board a ship bound for Shanghai. The year was 1863, and Ito was

Ito Hirobumi was one of the first Japanese to learn about the West first hand. In 1863, when he was twenty-two, the lord of his province of Choshu sent him on a secret mission to Europe, in defiance of the law forbidding foreign travel.

twenty-two years old. In Shanghai he signed on as a crewman on another ship and worked his way to London. The next year he received news that his lord the daimyo had ordered shore guns to fire on foreign ships entering the narrow straits between the islands of Honshu and Kyushu. Young Ito had learned enough about the West to know that that was a reckless action and hurried home to advise the daimyo to seek more peaceful means of dealing with the foreigners.

As Ito predicted, the guns on the Western ships easily destroyed the Japanese guns on shore. Being right did not make Ito any more popular with the older samurai, who were advising resistance to the foreigners no matter what. Several attempts were made on his life. On one occasion he was pursued into a teahouse, where a young woman hid him under the floorboards of her room. This adventure led to a closer acquaintance, and in time Ito married his rescuer.

Meanwhile the destruction of the shore guns served as a convincing demonstration of the necessity of adopting Western weapons. Ito was sent to Nagasaki to break the law again by arranging to import British guns. He was assisted in this assignment by representatives of the domain of Satsuma, where the samurai had learned a similar lesson. By March, 1866, the two domains had concluded a secret alliance to help each other to replace the shogun's government with a new government under the emperor. Ito's influence in the nation was growing steadily.

In September, 1866, after a rule of only eight years, the fourteenth shogun died and was succeeded by the fifteenth and last of the Tokugawa shoguns. In 1867, the emperor died. His heir was fourteen years old. On January 3, 1868, troops of Satsuma and Choshu seized the Imperial Palace in Kyoto. Their leaders convened an imperial council to rule the country, including as members no one who favored continuing the title of shogun. The shogun himself accepted the situation. The daimyo of some provinces did not and tried to resist the troops of Satsuma and Choshu, but to no avail. By April, 1868, the Tokugawa shogun was left as just one among many daimyo. Two-and-a-half centuries of Tokugawa rule were ended.

The council declared that the emperor was restored to his ancient power. It was customary to give every reign a new name. This one was given the name Meiji, meaning "illustrious rule." The "Meiji Restoration" was one of the most

*In January 1868, the lords of the provinces of Choshu and Satsuma seized
the capital city Kyoto and ended the long rule of the Tokugawa shoguns.
Their intent was to "restore" power to the emperor, who had long played
only a ceremonial role in government. Since these lords had Western arms
(shown here), resistance to the Restoration was short lived.*

significant events in the history of Japan, as it led to swift
and enormous changes throughout the nation.

6

A Rich Nation, A Strong Army

A strong Japan was the goal of the leaders of the Meiji Restoration of 1868. They sought to have all Japanese unite as loyal subjects of the emperor, whom they wanted to restore to a position of power in the nation after centuries as a figurehead. But the emperor was only fifteen years old, and had been emperor for only a year, since January, 1867. For a while at least the leaders of the Restoration would have to set policy for the nation, in place of the shogun's government that they had overthrown.

In April, 1868, the new imperial council, which these leaders had convened, issued a statement of the principles that would guide the new government. This statement, made in the name of the emperor, was called "The Charter Oath." It promised that policy would be formed after "public discussion," and urged that all classes should unite "in vigorously promoting the economy and welfare of the na-

*In April 1868, just after the Restoration of power to the emperor, an
imperial council issued a statement of the principles that would guide the
new government. Here the Emperor Meiji, age fifteen, listens to a
reading of this statement, the Charter Oath.*

tion," and that knowledge should "be sought throughout the
world."

In the spring of 1869, the emperor and his court moved
east from Kyoto to Edo, recognizing the fact that the nation
had long been ruled from the town that Ieyasu had made his
capital. Edo was renamed Tokyo, which means "Eastern

Capital." The palace of the Tokugawa shoguns now became the imperial palace.

The old slogan of those who favored rule by the emperor, "Honor the emperor, expel the barbarians," was now obsolete. The "barbarians" from the West were the source of much of the knowledge that was to be sought to strengthen Japan. A new slogan was adopted: "A rich nation, a strong army." Western nations had become rich and strong after throwing off the old feudal system of serfs and knights and barons. Japan still had its feudal system of peasants and samurai and daimyo. Many of the daimyo and samurai were deeply in debt to wealthy merchants, and the central government was also in debt.

The imperial council proposed that the daimyo give all the lands they controlled to the emperor, "so that uniform rule may prevail throughout the empire." The peasants cultivating the land would pay a tax to the central government. The government would guarantee the daimyo an income, and their debts would be taken over by the government. This proposal was accepted, and the lands were divided into seventy-two "prefectures" governed by officials appointed by the central government.

The members of the imperial council showed considerable political skill in introducing these changes, proceeding gradually by persuasion and example. Most of the changes were accepted peacefully. In a short time the council seemed well on the way to achieving the goal, "A rich nation." The new strength of the government inspired confidence for commerce. And the newly admitted foreign trade was a source of wealth.

One change that was not accepted peacefully involved the goal, "A strong army." The leaders of the Meiji Restoration had risen to power largely as a result of their success in building up the military strength of their own provinces, by copying Western military techniques. They knew how strong the Western nations were. They were especially aware of the defeats China had suffered.

That vast nation was in the process of being "carved up like a melon" by the nations of Europe, who were establishing "spheres of influence" in various provinces of China. There they were carrying on trade with little control from the Chinese government. The imperial council was determined that Japan would not lose control of its own affairs in that way.

The traditional defenders of Japan, of course, were the samurai. They were numerous still—the samurai and their families numbered about two million people, six percent of the national population. But samurai swords and samurai courage, remarkable as they were, had proved no match for Western-style armies. The imperial council resolved to create Western-style forces for the whole nation.

When the daimyo turned over their lands to the emperor, their troops, including their samurai, came under the control of the imperial council. The council incorporated these men into the national forces. But, said the council, every young Japanese had a responsibility to defend his country. There would be "universal military service." Under a law of January, 1873, any male could be called at age twenty-one for three years of active duty and six years in the reserve forces. Promotion in this national military force would be strictly on the basis of ability, with no distinction made between the samurai and the "commoners." That was a change many of the samurai could not accept.

Although in the long era of peace many samurai had found new occupations in government and trade, they were still proud of their samurai status. The visible symbols of that status were the two swords that only the samurai had the right to wear. In 1876, the imperial council decided that those symbols were inappropriate if all men were to have an equal right to advancement. The council banned the wearing of swords.

In 1877, a great samurai of Satsuma, Saigo Takamori, who earlier had played an active part in the Meiji Restoration, led an army in a revolt against the imperial council.

Saigo Takamori, a great samurai of Satsuma province, helped bring about the Meiji Restoration of 1868. But by 1877, he felt the new government had made too many changes, and he headed a revolt. After several months of heavy fighting, the government's army, drafted from all classes, defeated Saigo's samurai forces. The end of the revolt was also the end of the official status of the samurai as a class apart.

His purpose, he said, was to rescue the emperor from the "evil advisers" who were making so many changes in Japan—in Saigo's view changes for the worse. Casualties in the revolt totaled thirty thousand. Fighting lasted for six months. But the national army, drafted from all classes, defeated Saigo's samurai. Saigo asked a friend to behead him on the battlefield, which he did.

Saigo's defeat marked the end of official samurai status in Japan. But no government could force the samurai to forget that they were samurai, or persuade the Japanese people to forget the glorious warriors that had been a part of national life for so many centuries. A statue of Saigo with his faithful dog is a landmark in Tokyo today. The samurai spirit, *bushido*, literally "the way of the warrior," would play a part in Japanese history for many decades to come.

The imperial council's belief in advancement on the basis of ability was not applied only to the military forces. The council gave "commoners" some rights they had not had under the daimyo: to choose where they would live, to choose what occupation they would pursue, and to take a family surname. To help them advance and make a contribution to a strong modern Japan, the council introduced a plan to establish fifty-four thousand elementary schools—one for each six hundred Japanese. (As a result, half a century later Japan was the most literate nation in Asia.) A statement of educational goals—obedience, benevolence, service to the nation—called the "Rescript on Education" served as the fundamental ethical code of Japan until World War II. Promising students were sent to study at universities in other countries. Teachers from many Western nations were paid large salaries to come to Japan to teach Western subjects.

A strong, rich nation required modern industries, to build ships and weapons and to convert natural resources into goods that could be sold. The imperial council set about building factories and running them. The results were disappointing, in comparison with the achievements of the enterprises run by private citizens—by the great Mitsui family, for example. In 1881, the Minister of Finance suggested that the government-built industries be sold to private owners. This was done, and the industries began to flourish. Some of the buyers were the great old families, but most were new entrepreneurs.

One of the most successful was Iwasaki Yataro, who as a young man, in the years before the Meiji Restoration, had helped develop Western-style military forces in the province of Tosa. He used his government connections to enter the shipping business, and in time built his Mitsubishi Ship-

Business prospered under the new government. This Tokyo street scene from the 1870s shows two department stores and (center) the Western-style main office of the Mitsui Bank. The huge Mitsui corporation was one of the greatest of the zaibatsu, "financial cliques" favored by the government.

ping Company into a financial empire second in wealth only to the Mitsui Company. Then Iwasaki merged his shipping company with one owned by Mitsui and so gained even more power in Japan's economy.

The name given to these huge enterprises was zaibatsu, meaning "financial cliques." The imperial council's prime concern for the new industries was that they should grow to enrich the nation, and the government gave the zaibatsu all encouragement and cooperation. Cooperation between government and privately owned companies is one of the most distinctive characteristics of the Japanese economy today.

The money that the new industries earned was spent for the most part on expansion. Very little of the new wealth was passed along to the men and women who worked in the in-

Once Japan was reopened to foreign trade, Western technology was quickly adopted for commercial as well as military purposes. This rail line between Tokyo and Yokohama was completed in 1872.

dustries. Wages were low. But there were plenty of workers because of what was happening to the former peasants. The tax that they were required to pay on the production of their farms was the principal source of income for the new government. The government's program was ambitious and expensive; therefore the tax on the farmers was high. Many of the farmers simply could not produce enough to pay the tax and still feed their families. Some sold their land and became tenant farmers—"sharecroppers" they would be called in the United States. Many left their villages and went to the cities to work in industry.

In the traditional ranking of Japanese society, the farmers were just below the samurai, since agriculture was recognized as the source of the nation's wealth. They were no more happy about the change in their status brought about by the Meiji Restoration than the samurai were. But they did not revolt as the samurai led by Saigo had done, in part because for centuries they had been accustomed to obey the government and its officials. In addition, some Japanese who had studied Western ways were now talking about another way the people could influence their officials. It was called representative government—rule by representatives of the people.

Since the Meiji Restoration, the imperial council had been ruling the country in the name of the emperor. But the men who made up the council knew that one of their chief responsibilities was to develop a new form of government suitable for a new Japan. Above all, the emperor was to be the head; that was the purpose of the Meiji Restoration. Building the structure of his government required careful consideration, and training the men who would be part of it required time.

In 1881, the council announced that a form of representative government would be established by 1890 and sent Ito Hirobumi and others to Europe to study various governments there.

It was Ito's third trip to Europe. His first, in 1863, at age twenty-two, had been the secret and illegal mission to bring to his province of Choshu Western military technology. At age thirty he had been one of a group of one hundred seven officials and students sent around the world by the imperial council to improve Japanese relations with other countries. He was, therefore, one of the men in the government with the most first-hand experience with the West. Since 1873, he had been Minister of Public Works in the central government, and now at age forty he was well on his way to being its leading statesman.

Ito visited various countries governed by some combination of a sovereign and a legislature—the so-called "constitutional monarchies." He stayed longest in Germany. The

In 1871 the imperial council sent a delegation of 107 officials and students overseas to improve relations with the United States and European countries. Ito Hirobumi was one of the 107. This Japanese painting shows their departure from Yokohama.

legislature there, the Diet, was clearly under the control of the emperor, Kaiser Wilhelm I, and his powerful chancellor, Count Otto von Bismarck. Since no one in Japan had had any experience in representative government, Ito felt it would be wise to limit the power of a Japanese legislature in a similar way. He also liked the English idea of having two branches of the legislature, with a House of Lords made up of members of a hereditary nobility, as a cautious counterbalance to the elected representatives of the people in the House of Commons.

Back home in Japan, Ito played the leading role in drafting a constitution for Japan, which the emperor presented to the people in 1889—as it happened a hundred years after the Constitution of the United States was adopted. The new government had a legislature, called the *kokkai* or Diet, with a House of Peers (mostly members of the old nobility) and a House of Representatives. The two houses had equal authority, but were subordinate to the executive branch of government, the Cabinet of Ministers, which was in turn subordinate to the emperor. Not surprisingly, the ministers who made up the cabinet were for the most part the same men who had made up the imperial council. They were no doubt better qualified than most for these posts. Certainly Ito had earned the title he acquired in 1892: prime minister.

7
Japan
a Power in
the Far East

 When Ito Hirobumi became prime minister of Japan in August 1892, nearly twenty-five years had passed since the Meiji Restoration had ended the rule of the shoguns. In that quarter of a century Japan had made great strides in modernization and westernization. She had developed industry, established foreign trade, built a strong army and navy, and replaced the three-hundred-year-old government of the shoguns with a constitutional monarchy. These developments brought many benefits. But even modern Western nations have their problems, and Japan soon shared in them.

One goal of the new government was soon realized. Great Britain promised in 1894 that she would revise her treaty with Japan to remove the provision for extraterritoriality—effective in 1899, when the new codes of law being drafted in Japan would be in force. Other nations followed Britain's example.

True representative government was more difficult to achieve. Membership in the first political parties was based on loyalty to this leader or that one, rather than on loyalty to particular beliefs about government. There were many stormy sessions in the House of Representatives. That body was frequently dissolved and new elections held. Prime Ministers changed often. It was fortunate for Japan that the Cabinet of Ministers was still firmly in control of the government. The older leaders of the Meiji Restoration had now largely turned power over to the next generation, to men of the age of Ito Hirobumi. The emperor had promised in the Charter Oath of 1868 that policy would be decided "after public discussion." The House of Representatives held lengthy discussions, but it was the Cabinet of Ministers that did the deciding.

"A rich nation, a strong army" was still the motto. Foreign trade and modern industry had done much to make Japan richer, but there were limits to growth, as many another nation had found out. Specifically, Japan's islands provided a limited supply of raw materials for industry, so she had to buy them from other nations. In addition, wages were still so low in Japanese factories that few workers could afford to buy the goods being made. Therefore, if her industry was to expand, Japan had to buy raw materials abroad, bring them to Japan for manufacture, and then sell the products abroad. But England, another island nation, had a similar situation and managed it so successfully that she built a worldwide empire. One Japanese visitor to England remarked on the fact that he saw no fields growing crops; they had all been taken over by factories. Other small nations— Holland and Belgium—and some larger, more self-sufficient ones—Germany and France—were also building empires. Even the vast United States was discussing plans for expansion. It was the Age of Imperialism. In the minds of the leaders of the great imperial powers, it was clearly in the best interest of less developed nations to trade with them, and so receive the benefits of the latest in modern progress.

If those nations could not see that for themselves, then they must be shown. That had been the mission of British gunboats in China in 1840 and of Commodore Perry's "black ships" in Japan in 1853.

For Japan, the logical place to look for raw materials and larger markets was on the continent of Asia. The nearest major source of iron and coal was China's province of Manchuria, in the northeast corner of the nation, bordering on Russian Siberia and the kingdom of Korea. The nearest major market was Korea, occupying a peninsula that jutted out from the Asian continent toward Japan. If everyone would cooperate, Japan could buy raw materials in Manchuria, ship them to Japan, and pay for them with goods sold in Korea.

Everyone would not cooperate. Japan had learned that in 1876, when she requested trading rights in Korea. Korea, like all the other nations bordering on China, had for centuries given its allegiance to the Chinese emperor, in return for a promise of protection from attack by other nations. And China was not at all pleased with the way Japan had adopted Western ways, forsaking the wisdom of Confucius and Buddha. Japan was growing stronger, while China, forced to yield to many demands of Western nations, was growing weaker. Therefore, the king of Korea, out of loyalty to China, refused to grant the trading rights Japan requested.

Japan then demonstrated she had learned another Western way. She sent a squadron of warships to the Korean coast. The king soon agreed to grant the rights and signed a treaty with Japan that declared among other things that Korea was an independent nation. China protested the treaty, ineffectively. That had happened in 1876.

In 1894, a revolt broke out against the king of Korea. The king asked China for help, and Chinese troops arrived in Seoul. The Japanese government protested that this was a violation of Korea's independence and also sent troops to Korea, with the announced intention of ending Chinese interference in Korean affairs. That action startled the world: little Japan was defying great China. But the stakes were high: Japan sought free access to the continent of Asia. When China refused to give up her right to control Korea, Japan declared war.

The war was warmly supported by the Japanese people. The Western-style Japanese army quickly gained control of all Korea, and then, pressing on for victory, crossed the Yalu River into Manchuria. In February 1895, Japanese forces landed in another Chinese province, Shantung, and threatened to march on Peking. At that point China had to ask for peace.

In the Treaty of Shimonoseki, signed in April 1895, China acknowledged that Korea was an independent nation, promised to pay a large sum of cash to Japan as indemnity for the war, and ceded to Japan the Liaotung peninsula in Manchuria and the island of Taiwan. For China it was a disaster. Defeat by Japan demonstrated to the world how weak China really was. The Western nations increased their demands for privileges in China.

For Japan, and for Prime Minister Ito, the Treaty of Shimonoseki was, of course, a great victory. It increased Japan's prestige in the world enormously. But rejoicing in Tokyo was to be short. The European nations did not welcome the rise of a strong new nation in Asia. Japan had opposed China. Next she might oppose their plans for extending their empires. Immediately, in April, 1895, Russia, France, and Germany sent word to Prime Minister Ito that they feared Japanese control of the Liaotung peninsula was a threat to peace in the area, and they "advised" that it be returned to China. Their action is known to history as "the Triple Intervention." No one believed that their primary concern was peace, any more than Japan's primary concern had been the independence of Korea. But they were

Japan's continued economic growth depended on trade with the mainland of Asia. China resisted such trade, and in 1894 Japan declared war. In February 1895, the Japanese torpedoed and sank three large Chinese warships moored at Weihaiwei in Shantung province. Their loss led to the surrender of the Chinese fleet, and thus to Japanese victory over mighty China.

three powerful nations, and Japan was not yet ready to defy them. Victory turned to humiliation as Ito agreed to take their "advice." And the resentment caused by the intervention led to further strengthening of Japan's military forces, so that she would be able to resist such pressure in the future.

Five years later, Japanese troops were back in China, and this time their presence was warmly welcomed by the Western nations. For a long time many patriotic Chinese had been distressed by the ever-growing influence of foreigners in China. A whole section of the capital city, Peking, was set aside for representatives of other nations and their families. Christian missionaries were establishing churches, schools, and hospitals in towns and villages. While Chinese statesmen discussed how to stop the growth of foreign influence in China, a group of impatient men decided to take direct action. They called themselves "the Society of the Righteous Fists," which the Westerners soon shortened to "the Boxers." In 1899, the Boxers began raiding mission stations in the countryside out from Peking, burning the buildings, killing Chinese converts, and sometimes killing the missionaries. The missionaries fled for protection to Peking, to the legations of their various nations. Their diplomats protested the raids to the Chinese government, which replied that it deeply regretted the situation, but it was unable to control the Boxers. By June, 1900, the Boxers had surrounded the Legation Quarter in Peking, and begun a siege that was to last fifty-five days.

When the Western nations and Japan saw that the Chinese government could not, or would not, protect the men, women and children in the legations, they organized an international military force in Tianjin, the port for Peking. The orders to the force were simple: "Relieve the legations." On August 14, the international force entered Peking and put an end to what was called the Boxer Rebellion. In this action Japanese troops fought side by side with European and United States troops and earned considerable respect for their fighting effectiveness and their proper military conduct.

One nation was noticeably absent from the international rescue force: Russia. She had joined readily with France and Germany in the Triple Intervention of 1895 to force Japan out of Manchuria, saying Japan's presence was a threat to peace. The Boxer Rebellion was clearly a threat to peace, also. Russia chose to deal with it by occupying all the province of Manchuria, while the Chinese government's attention was engaged by the Boxers. In this way Russia furthered her most immediate objective in the area, which was to complete a railroad from Moscow to the Pacific. Russia's Pacific port free of ice for the longest season was Vladivostok. And the shortest, most direct route for a railroad from Moscow to Vladivostok lay across Manchuria.

Now it was Japan's turn to protest. Russian occupation of Manchuria threatened Japan's plans there and might affect her dealings with neighboring Korea as well. Japan was joined in the protest by the mightiest nation of all at that time, Great Britain. Britain was eager to prevent Russia from gaining too much influence in China's affairs. After delicate negotiations, Japan and Britain signed a treaty that provided that each would remain neutral if the other became involved in a war with another nation in the Far East. But if two or more nations attacked Japan or Great Britain, each would come to the aid of the other.

Japan's treaty with Britain greatly strengthened her position in all her foreign affairs. It was signed in 1902, and three months later Russia agreed to withdraw from Manchuria. A year later, however, the Russian troops were still there. Russia insisted that she had special rights in Manchuria. But when Japanese diplomats in Russia tried to get the Russians to admit that Japan had special rights in Korea, they refused. On February 6, 1904, the Japanese diplomats broke off the discussions of these matters. That same day both nations switched from diplomatic action to military action. The Russians sent troops across the Manchurian border into Korea, and the Japanese sent warships to Korea and to Manchuria. In Korea the ships landed Japanese army units that quickly occupied Seoul. In Manchuria, at Port Arthur, the night of February 8, Japanese destroyers surprised two Russian battleships and a cruiser at anchor and damaged them with torpedoes. On February 10, Japan declared war on Russia. The Russians, despite their own land action in Korea, criticized the Japanese for a sneak attack on their navy. But Japan's friends praised her "daring" action.

The Russo-Japanese War lasted for a year and a half. It

was watched with great interest by all the major nations. It was the first war in modern times between an Eastern and a Western nation. Its battles involved huge armies, of a size rarely seen before anywhere. And it was clear that the outcome would decide the future of Asia for years to come.

Russia was at a disadvantage in the war because reinforcements had to travel great distances to reach the scene of the fighting. By the end of May, 1904, the Japanese had pushed the Russian forces out of Korea, back into Manchuria, and had also landed near Port Arthur. They laid siege to the heavily fortified Russian base there, which held out until the last day of December. In February, 1905, they sent four hundred thousand men into action near the city of Mukden, against nearly as many Russians. The battle lasted for three weeks, with the Japanese finally winning the city, at a cost of forty thousand dead or wounded. These terrible battles were conducted with the most careful respect for military discipline and etiquette. The soldiers of the czar and the sons of the samurai came to view each other as worthy adversaries, and the commanders exchanged compliments back and forth.

In May, 1905, forty Russian warships arrived in Asian waters. They had set out from the Baltic Sea seven months before, to end Japanese control of the sea routes to Manchuria. A Japanese fleet met them in the straits between Japan and Korea, and after two days of fighting, only two of the forty Russian ships remained in action.

This great Battle of Tsushima Straits decided the war. Japan had paid a heavy price in men and money for her victories on land and sea and was as ready as Russia for peace. The Japanese asked the American President Theodore Roosevelt to be the mediator for a settlement to end the war. He arranged a peace conference in August in Portsmouth, New Hampshire, and the Treaty of Portsmouth was signed September 5, 1905.

In the treaty, Russia recognized at last that Japan had a special interest in Korea. More than that, Russia agreed to

The government slogan "a rich nation, a strong army" led to a requirement of military service for all young men. As the twentieth century opened, even school children were drilled with rifles.

transfer to Japan the leases that she had negotiated with China in Manchuria, along with the South Manchurian Railway linking Port Arthur with Mukden. And she ceded to Japan the southern half of Sakhalin Island, located between Siberia and Japan. Of the three territories mentioned, only Sakhalin Island actually belonged to Russia. What was important was that she agreed, in effect, not to compete with Japan in Asia.

China was unable to oppose the transfers in Manchuria. As for Korea, what Japan wanted was to stimulate and con-

trol the economic development of the country. Ito Hirobumi believed that peaceful pressure could achieve this goal,
while some military men in the Cabinet of Ministers advocated a direct takeover of the country. Ito's method was tried
for a time, but in 1909, a Korean assassin ended the career of
this great negotiator. His voice of moderation was now absent
from the cabinet, and military men dominated the government. The first result was the outright annexation of Korea as
a part of the Japanese empire—using as a pretext the assassination of Ito.

In two wars, only ten years apart, Japan had extended her
territory until it stretched from the island of Taiwan in the
south to the middle of Sakhalin in the north. And the military strength she had demonstrated had made it possible for
her to seize Korea without a fight and gain a free hand in the
economic development of Manchuria. These successes
greatly swelled the pride and ambition of the Japanese people. In forty years, the patriotic devotion to the emperor expressed in the Meiji Restoration had turned into a desire for
empire building as strong as that of any imperialist Western
nation. The slogan "A rich nation, a strong army" now had
an edge of menace.

The army was strong now, all right, and its leaders were
heroes in the eyes of the Japanese people. The balance in
government between the emperor's civilian and military advisors, which Ito Hirobumi had maintained for so long, was
now badly tilted. Ito was dead, and in 1912, the Emperor
Meiji died. His son had nowhere near his ability or influence. Soon after the emperor's death, when the Cabinet of
Ministers refused an army request for money for two additional divisions, the military forced the formation of a new
cabinet, with a prime minister who would cooperate with
the generals and admirals. From that time on, the military
often named the cabinets. Since the Diet was subordinate to
the cabinet, representative government for Japan ended, for
all practical purposes, before it was ever really tried.

In August, 1914, war broke out in Europe, a war that came to be called the First World War. Great Britain called on her ally Japan to help in a limited way by destroying the German warships that had been protecting German interests in China. Japan's military leaders thought that assignment much too small. They chose to go all out in the war, in hopes of increasing Japan's influence in Asia still further. They demanded, therefore, that Germany hand over to Japan the territory she had leased in Shantung province in China, and either withdraw her warships or disarm them. When Germany ignored these demands, Japan declared war. The European nations were still reluctant to have Japan gain more power in Asia, where they still had many plans of their own, but they were too occupied with the war to do much about it. They did suggest that Japan could help in the war by sending troops to Europe to fight, but Japan was interested only in Asia. She sent troops to Shantung province to take the German naval station at Tsingdao and the ships there. After that her major contribution to the war was providing munitions and shipping for Great Britain and her allies—services for which she was well paid. The disruption of normal trade between Europe and the Orient also provided Japan an opportunity to build up new markets for her exports.

The war also seemed to provide an opportunity for Japan to improve her position in China. The generals, the admirals, and the foreign minister drew up a list of what they would like from China. Their "Twenty-one Demands" included transferring Germany's lease in Shantung to Japan, extending Japan's leases in Manchuria for ninety-nine years, and giving Japan the right to name advisers to the Chinese government.

China was in a weaker position than ever when these demands were presented to her in 1915. The Empress Dowager Tzu-hsi, who had ruled China for forty-seven years, had died in 1908. In 1911, the man called the "George Washington of

China," Sun Yat-sen, had launched a revolution that had overthrown the dynasty of the Manchu emperors, but had not yet succeeded in establishing a stable government to rule the vast country. Sun's government signed an agreement granting Japan all she asked except the right to name advisers, but made it clear that the agreement was signed "under duress"—that is to say since undue pressure forced its signing, China maintained it should not be considered binding.

China, weak as she was, had taken part in the World War by sending noncombatant laborers to Europe to release Allied troops for fighting. Both Japan and China were represented, therefore, at the Peace Conference at Versailles in 1919 that attempted to work out all the conflicting claims of the nations that had fought. At the conference American President Woodrow Wilson presented his plan for a League of Nations that would hear such claims in the future, before they resulted in war. The League was set up, and Japan became a member. China's representatives requested that the Peace Conference cancel Japan's lease in Shantung, but their request was not granted. China did not sign the Treaty of Versailles, as a result. In addition, this ignoring of China's right to control her own territory was condemned by many people in the United States and was one reason the United States did not join the League of Nations.

Much trouble lay ahead. But when the League met for the first time in 1920, there was an optimistic feeling among the members. The war just ended had as one of its slogans "The War to End All Wars." Germany, viewed as the example of military expansion, had been defeated. Now the world could be ruled by a "law of nations," and governments could be spared the heavy expense of maintaining huge armies and navies. To work out the details of reducing their armed forces in a safe, orderly way, the representatives of nine nations—France, Italy, Great Britain, Belgium, the Netherlands, Portugal, the United States, China and Japan—

*After the First World War, the governments of nine major nations,
including Japan, resolved to find a way to escape the heavy expense of
maintaining large armies and navies. Their representatives met in 1921 in
Washington, D.C., for a disarmament conference.*

met in 1921 in Washington, D.C., for a Disarmament Conference.

A number of treaties and resolutions resulted from the
Washington Conference. Two were of special importance to
Japan. She agreed with Great Britain and the United States
on future naval strength. The two Western nations would
each have one major naval base in the Pacific, at Singapore
and Honolulu. The three nations would reduce the number
of their battleships, keeping their existing relative strength,
which was a ratio of five:five:three. That is to say for every
five battleships Britain kept, the United States would keep
five also, and Japan would keep three. Second, Japan agreed

to withdraw her troops from Shantung. This she promptly did.

The Japanese people had received with fierce pride the news of their nation's victories in the Sino-Japanese and Russo-Japanese wars. But by the 1920s they were ready for some peaceful triumphs. Most especially they wanted to continue the profitable trade they had developed in Asia during the World War. The political party founded by Ito Hirobumi, the Seiyukai, still stood for Ito's ideal of moderation. Its members in the House of Representatives, along with the Cabinet of Ministers, worked closely with the great corporations, the zaibatsu, in furthering economic growth. Too closely, some said, for some of the ministers had family ties to the corporations, and some of the elected representatives were caught selling their votes. It was not a time, however, of great moral scruples. The spirit that produced in the United States "The Roaring Twenties" and the "Jazz Age" was present in Japan, too. Girls in Tokyo wore the "flapper" dresses popular in the West, and cafes and nightclubs flourished.

The enormous vitality of Japan at this time is indicated by the speed with which the nation recovered from a terrible natural disaster. On September 1, 1923, a great earthquake struck Tokyo and nearby Yokohama. Fires broke out, and a brisk wind spread them throughout the wooden buildings of both cities. Yokohama was almost completely destroyed, and half of Tokyo, a city of four million, was devastated. One hundred thirty thousand people died. Many nations sent disaster aid, and, amazingly, four years later the ruined cities of wood had been replaced by thriving cities of steel and concrete.

The "boom times" of the 1920s did not benefit everyone equally, of course. Prices rose, but wages did not rise enough to keep pace. This provided an opportunity for the critics of capitalism, the Socialists, to recruit members for new political parties. Dissatisfaction and genuine hardship led to demonstrations, even riots against the government. And the government had not yet developed democratic ways strong enough to deal with dissent. It reacted by sending police to knock the heads of the demonstrators and by passing laws providing severe punishments for "dangerous thought." The elementary schools, which almost every Japanese child now attended, were charged with teaching proper thoughts about the nation. Now the government added to that early indoctrination a year of compulsory military service for boys, where Japanese virtues could be further taught. For despite the surface prosperity of the decade, and despite widespread corruption, there were still those Japanese who remembered the old ways that had made Japan unique in the world. They had not forgotten the "way of the warrior," the way of the noble samurai who gladly died for honor—and for an emperor, alone among rulers of the world, descended directly from the gods.

In 1927, a new emperor ascended the throne. He was twenty-six years old. He had been carefully trained to rule, following the detailed instructions of his grandfather, the Emperor Meiji. His teacher in the old ways had been the general most responsible for Japan's victory in the war against Russia. But he had a modern education, too. He had visited Great Britain in 1921, and he had a scientific turn of mind, with a great interest in marine biology. The name chosen to designate his reign was "Showa," which means "enlightened peace." His personal name is Hirohito.

8

The Return
of the Samurai

Early 1927, when Hirohito became Emperor of Japan, was a time of public ceremonies and celebrations. It was also a time for many private discussions of the place of the emperor in the life of the nation. Sixty years before, the Meiji Restoration had overthrown the shogun's government to restore power to the emperor. He had governed at first in consultation with an imperial council of ministers. Twenty years later the idea of a constitutional monarchy had been introduced, and from then on the emperor governed in consultation with a Cabinet of Ministers and a legislature. At least, that was what the Constitution of 1889 said. But many Japanese saw that the country was actually being run by the leaders of a few political parties, supported by the great Japanese corporations, the zaibatsu. The parties used all sorts of means, including bribes, to get their candidates elected to the House of Representatives and to get their legislation passed. And the party leaders told the emperor the man he should name as prime minister to preside over the cabinet.

The government as it existed in 1927, some Japanese said, was quite different from the ideal the leaders of the Meiji Restoration had had in mind. The emperor seemed to have no more power now than in the centuries of rule by shogun—"the barbarian-subduing commander-in-chief." Furthermore, the shogun's government at its best had provided strong, stable government and had successfully resisted foreign influence. The backbone of the government then had been the loyal, courageous samurai with their code of *bushido*, "the way of the warrior." (These discussions forgot that the world in 1927 was a much more complicated place than the world of the shoguns. Many powerful nations had interests in Asia and would not allow Japan to isolate herself from the world. And wars were no longer won by individual courage. But it was easier to discuss the simple past than the complicated present.)

Such discussions of the proper place of the emperor often referred to a book called *A General Outline for the Reconstruction of Japan*, published in 1923 and promptly banned by the government. The author was Kita Ikki, a student of socialist political thought. His *General Outline* proposed that Japan be reconstructed as a socialist state, with private ownership of property abolished, and everything owned by the state. Just as the daimyo had turned over their domains to the emperor at the time of the Meiji Restoration, now the great corporations would turn over their factories, ships and so on to the government. Since they would not be likely to do that voluntarily, the "reconstruction" would have to be brought about by a coup d'etat, a takeover of the nation by the military, followed by a period of martial law. The strong Japan that would emerge could then easily conquer Manchuria and Siberia and other territories to gain the raw materials she needed for her industrial growth.

Kita's ideas were rejected, of course, by the moderate political leaders who were honestly trying to build a demo-

Emperor Hirohito inherited the rule of Japan when he was twenty-six, in 1927. He was proclaimed the 124th emperor of Japan, a direct descendant of the two gods that created the island nation thousands of years ago.

cratic government for Japan. And they were condemned by the zaibatsu whose property would be taken from them. But some of his ideas appealed to two groups of Japanese: To "superpatriots" who wanted Japan to be the absolute "master of Asia," rallying all the Oriental nations to drive out the Westerners and manage their own affairs. And to young military officers who, as always in times of peace, were frustrated by the inaction and slow promotion of service life in the 1920s. Some members of these groups spoke of "completing" the work of the Meiji Restoration. The era of the new emperor was designated "Enlightened Peace"—Showa. What was needed now, they said, was a "Showa Restoration"—the coup that would give the emperor and his government more power at home and abroad as had been proposed in Kita's *General Outline*.

While all this talk of extreme remedies was going on in private, Japan's government continued on its bumpy way. The two strongest political parties were the Seiyukai and the Kenseikai. Control of the government alternated back and forth between them in the mid-1920s. In 1927, soon after the Emperor Hirohito ascended the throne, the leader of the Seiyukai was named prime minister. He was a military man, General Tanaka Giichi.

Tanaka had a special interest in China. He had fought in the war with China in 1894, as a twenty-one-year-old graduate of Japan's Military Staff College. He had watched as Dr. Sun Yat-sen led the revolution in 1911 that overthrew the Chinese emperor and as he tried unsuccessfully to establish a democratic government in China. Now Japanese troops were routinely stationed in two Chinese provinces: Manchuria, to protect the railway won from Russia, and Shantung, to man the Tsingtao naval base taken over from Germany. Dr. Sun had died in 1925, and there was a new leader in China, a military man like Tanaka. What was more, he had taken his military training in Japan, which he had chosen to do because Japan offered the best and most difficult military courses in the Orient. This man, Tanaka realized, was different from the Chinese politicians and generals who had yielded so often to foreign demands. He must be carefully watched. His name was Chiang Kai-shek.

Sun Yat-sen had sought support for his new government for China from the leaders of the armies of the deposed emperor, in various provinces. While many had promised to help him, most had quickly turned their energies to building up their own power and had actually become independent rulers in the provinces. "Warlords" they were called. The result was that Dr. Sun's government in fact governed only one province, in the south of the nation.

Chiang Kai-shek's solution was to lead an army north to take control of China's key cities, rivers and rail lines. He

had trained his soldiers in modern tactics, and many of the
soldiers of the warlords came over to his side rather than
fight. That left the warlords a choice of following their men,
or fleeing. The farmers and the city workers welcomed
Chiang because they believed he would provide the im-
provement in their condition promised by Sun Yat-sen. The
month before General Tanaka became Prime Minister of
Japan, in March 1927, Chiang Kai-shek's troops entered
China's largest city, Shanghai, at the mouth of the Yangtze
River. The southern half of China was won, and control of
Shanghai and the Yangtze gave Chiang control of the na-
tion's economy.

The warlords of the northern provinces, led by the warlord of Manchuria, General Chang Tso-lin, joined forces to
resist. Prime Minister Tanaka did not expect them to suc-
ceed. Soon Chiang Kai-shek's army would be in Shantung
province. Would he respect the transfer of the lease on the
German naval base at Tsingtao? Would he respect the special rights granted to Japan in Manchuria? A month after
taking office, Prime Minister Tanaka sent two thousand additional troops to Tsingtao, hoping their presence would
stop Chiang Kai-shek's advance northward. Chiang's response was somewhat surprising. He never liked to risk his
troops in battle if he could accomplish his goals another way.
This time, he traveled to Japan and proposed that if the
Japanese would recognize his government as the legal government of China, he would recognize Japan's special rights
and interests in Manchuria.

Official recognition by Japan would greatly strengthen
Chiang Kai-shek's position, in China and in the world. But
a strong, united China was never what Japan wanted. Prime
Minister Tanaka refused the "deal" Chiang Kai-shek of-
fered. Chiang returned to China and the next year captured
Peking. And Prime Minister Tanaka sent more troops to
Tsingtao. They prevented Chiang from taking the capital
of Shantung province and then tried to take it themselves.
More than three thousand Chinese were killed in a bom-

bardment of the city. Japanese actions in Shantung led to several conclusions. Chiang Kai-shek saw that Japan was an enemy. Western nations saw that the Japanese military men, who had behaved so correctly in the Russo-Japanese War and at the time of the Boxer Rebellion, were capable of less admirable behavior. Most important, many young Japanese officers concluded that no matter what the politicians in Tokyo said about peace, the time of inaction was coming to an end.

Excitement ran especially high in military units in Manchuria. Young Japanese officers stationed there knew that Manchuria, with its natural resources and developed industries, was the richest prize in the Orient. They also felt they knew more than their superiors in Tokyo about how Japan could win that prize. Chiang Kai-shek's advance on Peking in the spring of 1928 seemed to give them an opportunity not to be missed, and they decided to act without waiting for approval from Tokyo.

The opportunity was this: the warlord of Manchuria, Chang Tso-lin, was returning home from Peking by train. The young officers planted a bomb that destroyed his rail car and killed him. While a successor was being chosen to rule Manchuria, they intended to step in and take control, saying that was necessary to protect Japanese property in the region. But such follow-up action required support for their plan from their superiors, and that was denied them.

Prime Minister Tanaka was not responsible for the assassination, and he sought punishment for those who were. Army headquarters in Tokyo, however, refused to punish the guilty officers, either for murder or for insubordination. It was a clear signal that the military was not under the control of the Cabinet of Ministers, and that military men could act on their own and get away with it. Independent actions by young officers soon multiplied.

The next year, 1929, boom times in Japan came to a halt, as an economic depression spread around the world. In the

United States of America, the stock market on Wall Street "crashed," banks failed, and many fortunes were wiped out. Japanese sales of raw silk to America, which had provided a good extra income for farmers, were cut in half—silk was a luxury fabric that people could do without in hard times. Many Japanese demanded that the government take action to improve conditions, but no one knew what was the right action to take. Some economic measures attempted actually made matters worse.

In the midst of all the discontent and hardship caused by the depression, the advocates of a Showa Restoration gained new followers. If Japan were "master of Asia," as they said she should be, then she would be less affected by decisions made in the West. As always, the rich Chinese province of Manchuria seemed the place to begin. The assassination of warlord Chang Tso-lin by the Japanese young officers had come to nothing because of the unwillingness of the politicians in Tokyo to follow up on the opportunity it presented to take over the province. The politicians must not be allowed to stand in the way any longer, said the advocates of the Showa Restoration.

Prime Minister Tanaka had resigned because of the refusal of the military high command to punish the men responsible for the assassination of Chang Tso-lin. His successor, Prime Minister Hamaguchi Yuko, also favored moderation rather than violence in dealing with Manchuria and China. In November, 1930, a young superpatriot shot Prime Minister Hamaguchi; he died a few months later. Early in 1931, a number of members of a patriotic society plotted a series of riots and bombings that would lead to the military takeover of the government as proposed in *A General Outline for the Reconstruction of Japan.* The plot was discovered, but again the plotters escaped punishment. By this time the members of the Cabinet of Ministers realized they could not control the military, and furthermore realized that their opposition to military proposals might put their own lives in danger. The young officers in Manchuria were now ready to act again.

On the night of September 18, 1931, near the Manchurian capital, Mukden, they set off some explosions that damaged slightly the Japanese-owned South Manchurian Railway. They accused some Chinese soldiers in the area of having caused the damage and said that in order to protect Japanese property it was necessary to seize the Mukden arsenal and airfield. The next day they took over the whole city, and two days later Japanese reinforcements entered Manchuria from Korea. By the end of the year, Japanese forces controlled all of Manchuria. In 1932, the Japanese army declared Manchuria was now an independent country—independent of China, that is—and set up a puppet government headed by the last Manchu emperor of China, who had been deposed in 1911.

The new ruler of China, General Chiang Kai-shek, was still consolidating his hold on the nation. The economic problems caused by the worldwide depression had been

In 1931, a Japanese army marched across the vast plain of Manchuria, China's rich northeastern province. As in the 1894 war, their purpose was to gain access to the raw materials and markets of Asia.

made worse in China by disastrous floods. And Chiang's political party, the Nationalist Party, was encountering growing opposition from the Chinese Communist Party, founded in 1921, and now under the vigorous leadership of Mao Zedong. Chiang Kai-shek considered Mao a country hick, but millions of peasants in China were listening to what he said about the still unfulfilled promises of Sun Yat-sen's revolution. Chiang, Mao pointed out, seemed much more interested in helping bankers and financiers than in helping farmers and workers. Chiang decided that he must destroy the communists in China before he could fight the Japanese in Manchuria. He appealed to the League of Nations for help against Japanese aggression. The League condemned Japan, which led to Japan's resignation from the League, but the member nations were too occupied with the problems of the depression to take any concrete action in Manchuria.

In Tokyo, the Cabinet of Ministers tried to stop the army's unauthorized seizure of Manchuria, but the generals replied that if they stopped short of complete control of the country, it would endanger the Japanese troops already there. Their plea—there is an "operational necessity" to continue— is an old trick of military men determined to avoid civilian control. It convinced many patriotic Japanese. In February, 1932, members of a patriotic society assassinated a former finance minister who opposed the Manchurian action, and a few weeks later they killed the head of the Mitsui Corporation, greatest of the zaibatsu, who had advocated making profits through peaceful progress, rather than through war. In May, another patriotic society launched another attack on government buildings, including the National Bank of Japan and Tokyo police headquarters, seeking again to make martial law a necessity. Their plan failed for lack of organization, but they did assassinate the new prime minister—the second prime minister slain in a year and a half.

At that point, when Emperor Hirohito asked his council of elder statesmen whom he should name as a replacement, they told him that no leader of a political party seemed able to form a cabinet that could govern the nation. They proposed that Japan return to the plan used before the parties grew strong: a "national unity" cabinet with ministers drawn from several parties, and a prime minister associated with no party. Recognizing reality, they suggested that the prime minister be a military man. Because they felt the navy was a bit better disciplined than the army, they proposed a navy man, Admiral Saito Makoto, who took office in May, 1932. The choice was acceptable to the army men. It was welcomed by the people of Japan, who were disgusted by the corruption they had seen in party governments and were cheering the army's achievements in Manchuria. By May, 1933, the army had added another Chinese province, Jehol, to the territory they controlled, and signed a truce with the Chinese that provided for a "demilitarized zone" (a strip of land without military units) between Peking and the Manchurian border. North of this buffer zone, the Japanese army paused to build up its strength.

The Tokyo cabinets that followed in the 1930s were all headed by military men and had fewer and fewer civilian ministers. The cabinets adopted a number of "emergency measures" to deal with the economic distress caused by the depression, calling on the people for hard work, thrift, and patriotism—qualities the Japanese excel in. By keeping wages low, and by reducing the value of the Japanese unit of money, the yen, relative to the money of other nations, they made Japanese products cheap in world markets and thus increased exports. By sending quantities of capital from Japan to develop further the mines and factories of Manchuria, they made that region the most highly industrialized area on the continent of Asia, with the greatest potential to further the old goal, "A rich nation, a strong army." As a result of these measures, involving considerable sacrifice by the Japanese people, Japan was the first major power to recover from the depression.

Manchuria's neighbor on the north was Russia, or rather,

since the Russian Revolution, the Union of Soviet Socialist Republics. The communist government there had made it clear it would oppose further Japanese expansion in Asia. In fact, it had formed an organization called the Communist International, shortened to "Comintern," that was advocating communist governments for all countries. If the communists in China gained more power, Manchuria, Korea, and even Japan itself would be "encircled," as some Japanese put it. The loudest voices opposing communist doctrine came from the Nazi Party in Germany and the Fascist Party in Italy, both working closely with industrialists in their countries. When Germany proposed that Japan join her in an "Anti-Comintern Pact"—an agreement to work together to stop the spread of communism—Japan quickly accepted the offer. The next year Italy also joined the Pact.

In China, Chiang Kai-shek was having little success with his plan to destroy the Chinese communists first and then fight the Japanese. Mao Zedong led his followers on an epic journey, now known as "The Long March," from the south of China to join other communists in the northwest. His rallying cry was "Head north to fight the Japanese." Another man urging resistance to Japan was the son of the assassinated warlord of Manchuria, known as "Young Marshal Chang," to distinguish him from his father. The Young Marshal had withdrawn his father's troops from Manchuria into China, expecting Chiang Kai-shek to help them win back their homeland. Five years later this had not happened.

As soon as Mao Zedong had established himself in the northwest, he proposed that Young Marshal Chang join him to fight the Japanese. For some months the Young Marshal did not say yes and did not say no. Then in December, 1936, Chiang Kai-shek ordered him to join in attacking the communists. That was too much for the Young Marshal. He decided on a drastic step. He kidnapped Chiang Kai-shek from his headquarters in the city of Xi'an and forced him to promise to unite with the communists to fight the Japanese.

His bold action succeeded. For four years China had a "United Front" against Japan.

When the Japanese high command heard of these developments in China, they began to analyze what effect they would have on Japan's plans to be "master in Asia." Some felt that Japan should push farther into China at once, before Chiang Kai-shek worked out a plan for cooperation with Mao Zedong. At the least, Japanese troops on the continent should be prepared for battle. For the third time in six years, a Japanese-owned railroad guarded by Japanese troops provided the setting for an incident.

This time it was the line running from Peking to its port of Tianjin. Historians disagree on whether this incident was planned by the Japanese or was simply the spark that was bound to flash as tension built as a result of China's growing strength. On the night of July 7, 1937, the commander of the Japanese rail guards asked the Chinese officer in charge of a village near Peking for permission to search the village for one of his men who was missing. The Chinese refused, a shot was fired. A skirmish followed between Chinese and Japanese troops at a nearby bridge, called the Marco Polo Bridge. Within a week, Japanese armies were invading China. Within a month, they had occupied Tianjin. Chiang Kai-shek abandoned Peking to them so that its historic art treasures would not be destroyed in the fighting. He made his first determined stand when the Japanese landed troops near Shanghai, seeking to control China's greatest port and the Yangtze River route to the interior of the country. Chiang's best units held the Japanese for three months, showing their countrymen and the world that the invaders were not invincible.

During that three months, the Japanese Army Air Force dropped bombs on Shanghai. A new kind of warfare was developing that was to involve civilians as well as soldiers in its destruction, in Asia and in Europe. Then the Japanese landed more troops, behind the Chinese defense lines, and Shanghai fell. The invaders moved up the Yangtze to Nanking, the city that Chiang had made the capital of China. He abandoned that city, too, and the Japanese thought the war was over. But Chiang quickly established a temporary capital four hundred miles upriver in the city of Hankou.

Hopes for an easy conquest of China ended at Nanking, with Chiang Kai-shek's refusal to give up the fight. The Japanese unit commanders who had captured the city were furious. The achievement they had planned as a knock-out blow that would send them home to a victory parade in Tokyo turned out to be just one more local success. Their soldiers in the ranks, many of whom had recently been called up from the reserves to fight in China, were frustrated, too. The officers lost all control of their men, who found an outlet for their emotions in brutal attacks on the civilians remaining in the city. Their "Rape of Nanking" resulted in the deaths of tens of thousands of Chinese and horrified the world. News of the atrocities was kept out of the papers in Japan.

It was clear that in time the Japanese could also take Hankou, and in October, 1938, they did. But in the meantime the Chinese set up a new base of operations in a place where the mountainous terrain made it impossible for Japanese tanks and warships to follow: Chongqing, in Sichuan province. In a marvelous show of determination, the Chinese dismantled whole factories, power plants, even universities, and moved them piece by piece to Chongqing. They did it on river boats, on pack animals, and on their backs. From this interior capital, Chiang continued the war.

Since Chiang Kai-shek would not come to terms with the Japanese, there remained the long task of winning control of China, city by city, province by province. The land was Chiang's ally, for the Japanese armies had to occupy the areas they conquered and that required many divisions in the third largest country in the world. To slow the Japanese advance across the plains in the east, Chiang called on the land again: he ordered the dikes that contained the Yellow River broken. The resulting floods wrecked Japanese strategy, but at a cost of thousands of Chinese drowned and thousands of farms destroyed. Chiang accused the Japanese of opening the dikes, and perhaps some of the grieving farmers believed him, but impartial observers knew the Japanese were too smart for such a self-defeating tactic. The Japanese commanders kept at their task. In October, 1938, an invasion in the south captured Canton. By the end of the year every major city in China was in Japanese hands. And still there was no victory.

The architects of the plan to make Japan master of Asia had seen China as their cornerstone. They intended to build on a conquered China an empire consisting of those countries which had looked to China for protection for centuries. But China in 1938 provided Japan no foundation for anything. The civilian population, loyal to Chiang Kai-shek or at least loyal to China, did everything they could to hinder Japanese activities. Many, especially Mao's communists, carried on expert guerrilla warfare against the Japanese even in the areas supposedly conquered. Much more important for Japan's future, however, was the world political situation in 1938.

By 1939, Japan had conquered all the eastern part of China, from Manchuria in the north to Hainan Island (above) in the south.

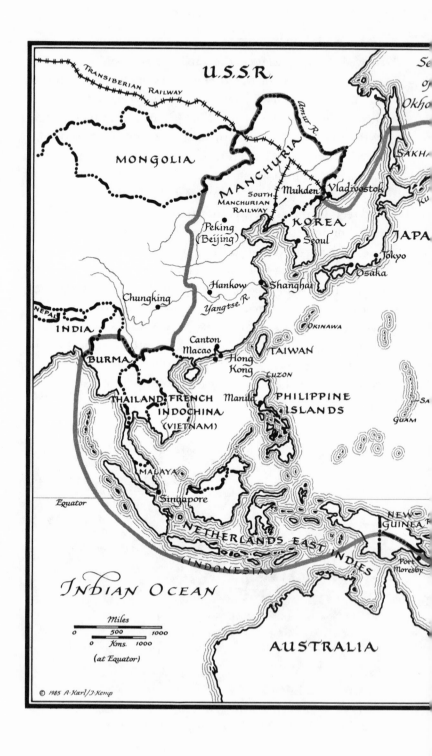

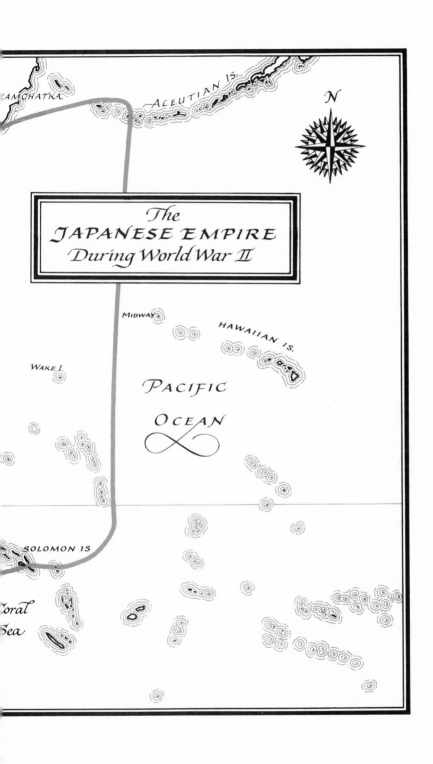

KAMCHATKA

ALEUTIAN IS.

N

The
JAPANESE EMPIRE
During World War II

MIDWAY

HAWAIIAN IS.

WAKE I.

PACIFIC

OCEAN

SOLOMON IS

Coral
Sea

9

A World at War

 In 1938, Nazi Germany, Japan's partner in the Anti-Comintern Pact, won control of Austria and part of Czechoslovakia. The next year Germany invaded Poland, causing Great Britain and France to declare war on Germany. The Nazi armies then overran France, Belgium, and Holland and stood poised to invade Britain.

The war in Europe seemed to give Japan a choice of opportunities. She could make a lot of money, as she had done in the First World War, by selling her products in the markets in Asia ordinarily supplied by the Europeans. This was the choice advocated by many of the civilian members of the Japanese government. But most of the military men in the government saw a larger opportunity. In addition to wider markets, Japan needed raw materials for her industries, especially for the war plants supplying her forces in China. The French colony in Vietnam (called French Indochina)

had rubber, the British colonies of Malaya and Burma had bauxite (for aluminum) and tin, and the Dutch colonies in the islands of the East Indies had oil. While the European colonial powers were fighting Germany, it was time, said these military men, for Japan to seize all those colonies—or rather, as they put it, to "free" them all from Western domination. Then Japan would indeed be master of Asia, and lead all Asiatics to a better life.

This second choice had a great attraction for many Japanese, appealing as it did to idealists seeking greater power for their divine emperor and to ordinary citizens pinched by the high taxes and low wages they had accepted for years for the good of the nation.

Not every military man in Japan considered the proposal a good one, however. Admiral Yamamoto Isoroku, probably the best naval strategist in the nation, was opposed to it. In 1939, Japan had the third strongest navy in the world. The strongest navy of all, that of Great Britain, was presently fighting the Germans. But the second strongest navy was not, Admiral Yamamoto pointed out to his colleagues. That was the navy of the United States of America. Yamamoto had served in Washington for two years as naval attaché in the Japanese embassy and had learned something about the way Americans think. They did not consider themselves a colonial power, yet they had acquired the Philippine Islands from Spain in 1898. A Japanese seizure of European colonies near the Philippines might bring that American fleet steaming across the Pacific. The American president, Franklin D. Roosevelt, had already moved the home base of the United States Pacific Fleet from California to Pearl Harbor in Hawaii. And Admiral Yamamoto knew that while he might win a number of naval battles, in a long war, the greater resources of the United States would give the Americans eventual victory. "Japan cannot beat America," he said in 1940. "Therefore Japan should not fight America."

The Japanese leaders had long discussions on what would

Admiral Yamamoto Isoroku was the best naval strategist of Japan in the 1930s. He warned that "Japan cannot beat America," because the United States had greater resources. But he obeyed orders and planned the naval attack on Pearl Harbor, December 7, 1941.

be the probable response of the Westerners, including the Americans, to the proposed seizure of the European colonies. No one could deny Admiral Yamamoto's point that the West had superior physical resources for a war. But many felt that Japan had a superior will to fight. The Westerners, they said, loved their comfort too much to make sacrifices to fight a war for very long, if indeed they took any action at all. There was, in fact, a long record of inaction to consider. Japan had already "freed" Korea and Manchuria from China's "domination" and had invaded China, and the Western nations had protested but done nothing. Italy, under the Fascist dictator Benito Mussolini, had invaded the African nation of Ethiopia and the Western nations had protested and done nothing. Even on the continent of Europe, Austria and Czechoslovakia had fallen under German control, thanks to the false promises that the Nazi dictator Adolf Hitler had made to the leaders of Great Britain and France, but it was not until Hitler invaded Poland that Great Britain and France declared war.

As for the United States, the leaders' discussions continued, Japanese observers reported that there was a feeling among a large part of the American population that what happened in the rest of the world was no business of theirs. The United States, these Americans said, was rich enough and strong enough to exist in "isolation" from the world, protected by an ocean on either side. And these "isolationists" had many powerful posts in the United States Congress, which would have to approve any participation in a war.

The advocates of seizing the colonies argued that any Western response would be so slow in coming that Japan would have time to consolidate her position. The territories seized would give her the resources Admiral Yamamoto worried about. Then the Japanese navy could form a "ring of steel" stretching from the North Pacific south almost to Australia. Japanese ships would be relatively close to their bases and could successfully take on all comers. On the other hand, these advocates said, if Japan did not act soon, she might not even be able to continue supporting her armies in China. She was buying a lot of oil and scrap iron for munitions from the United States, and President Roosevelt was urging that such sales be stopped.

In July, 1940, the Japanese leaders reached some decisions. They would see how much they could gain from the
colonial powers by diplomatic pressure. They would avoid
war, if possible, especially war with the United States. But if
there was no other way to ensure adequate supplies for their
armies and navy, they would go to war. The alternative—to
give up the idea of defeating Chiang Kai-shek and bring their
armies home from China—was unthinkable for them. Thus
the decision for war might be considered the result of the military man's old argument of "operational necessity" carried to
extreme lengths. Carried to the point of insanity, many said
later. But the decisions reached in July were ratified reluctantly by Emperor Hirohito in September.

Japanese diplomats went to work. They asked the French to
let Japan station troops in the northern half of Vietnam to
protect, they said, the southern flank of Japanese armies in
China. This request was granted. They strengthened the Anti-
Comintern Pact with Germany and Italy to make it a full
military alliance, announcing to the world the formation of
a "Rome-Berlin-Tokyo Axis." This assertion that Germany,
Italy and Japan had common interests in the world made even
the most complacent observers question Japanese intentions.

In November, 1940, the Americans elected Franklin
Roosevelt president for the third time—the only time they
ever elected one man for more than two terms as president.
He was an eloquent opponent of the Axis powers. The Japanese realized that the isolationists were losing strength in the
United States. The same month the Americans stopped
selling iron and steel to Japan. Oil might be next.

As protection against that possibility, the Japanese diplomats had asked the Dutch to agree to sell them most of the oil
produced in the East Indies. The Dutch delayed answering
through the fall of 1940 and the early months of 1941. It
seemed that diplomacy had accomplished all it could. War
was the next step. But the Japanese leaders still wanted to
avoid fighting the United States.

The United States ambassador to Tokyo for the past eight years, Joseph C. Grew, had a good knowledge of the country and wanted very much to avoid a war between Japan and the United States. In late 1940, the Japanese chose an ambassador to Washington with an equal desire to avoid war: Admiral Nomura Kichisaburo. Like Admiral Yamamoto, he had served as a naval attaché in Washington, and he had become acquainted with Franklin Roosevelt when Roosevelt was Assistant Secretary of the Navy. Grew and Nomura would ensure that diplomatic efforts for peace would continue. But Grew warned that it was quite possible for the Japanese to seek with all sincerity peaceful solutions for their problems and at the same time plan for war as an alternative.

In June, 1941, the Dutch finally replied to the Japanese request for oil from the East Indies. The reply was no. The Japanese prime minister met with other ministers and the military chiefs of staff. They decided that Japan must seize the European colonies, even if it did bring about war with the United States. In July, Japan sent troops into the southern half of Vietnam. The plan was to invade Malaya, knock out the great British naval base at Singapore at the tip of the Malay Peninsula, and then capture the islands of the Dutch East Indies.

The first move, into southern Vietnam, brought an immediate response from the United States. All trade with Japan was cut off. Ambassador Nomura tried to get that decision reversed. United States Secretary of State Cordell Hull told him that the United States would consider that only if Japan ceased its acts of aggression—and that meant withdrawing its troops from Vietnam and from China. The diplomats' room for negotiation was growing smaller and smaller.

The Japanese minister of war, General Tojo Hideki, and the chiefs of staff told the prime minister that the decision to attack could not be delayed beyond October, because of the dwindling stocks of oil. The prime minister and the few remaining civilian ministers resigned in October, and

General Tojo Hideki, Japanese Minister of War, was a leader of the military men who achieved control of the government in the 1930s. In October 1940, he acquired the additional post of Prime Minister.

a new cabinet was formed with military men in every seat. General Tojo became the new prime minister, but kept his title as minister of war as well. This new cabinet sent word to Ambassador Nomura in Washington that unless by the end of November Japan got a guarantee of a supply of oil, she would declare war. But the only concession they allowed him to offer as a bargaining point was a promise to withdraw from Vietnam.

Mention of the end-of-November deadline was intended for Ambassador Nomura's information only, not as an ultimatum to the United States. But United States intelligence agents had broken the Japanese diplomatic code and reported to Secretary of State Hull all messages sent to Nomura. Secretary Hull was an upright American brought up in the tradition of "Say what you mean and mean what you say." Ambassador Grew's warning that the Japanese could sincerely seek peace and plan war at the same time was hard for him to accept.

Of course, much planning was required if Japan was to launch an attack at the end of November. The most difficult assignment went to the Chief of the Combined Fleets, Admiral Yamamoto. It was nothing less than to prevent the United States Pacific Fleet from interfering with the attack plan. Yamamoto still believed that Japan should not fight America. But if his country decided otherwise, it was his duty to do everything possible to win. For months, therefore, he had been studying the enemy, working out a plan he hoped he would never have to use. It was a strategy the Japanese fleet had used successfully in 1904 against Russia, when Yamamoto was a young lieutenant. At the very beginning of the 1904 war, the Japanese had surprised two battleships and a cruiser at anchor at the Russian naval base at Port Arthur in Manchuria and damaged them with torpedoes. Now Yamamoto's plan was a surprise attack to knock out as much as possible of the United States Pacific Fleet on the first day of the war, using planes taking off from Japanese aircraft carriers. If the attack succeeded, the superior might of the Americans would be brought down closer to the strength of the Japanese fleet.

When Yamamoto presented his plan, his colleagues objected that the American warships were based halfway across the Pacific, in Hawaii. How would it be possible to take a major task force that far across open seas without its being noticed, they asked. And if it was noticed, the element of surprise, the element that gave Yamamoto his greatest advantage, would be lost. Yamamoto insisted there was a way to do it and continued studying the Americans—their schedules, the location of the docks and air fields, the mountains and bays around Honolulu.

In November Ambassador Nomura's negotiations in Washington made no progress, since each side was willing to yield so little. The Japanese chiefs of staff, advised by Admiral Yamamoto, concluded that the best day to launch their massive attack would be December 7. It was a Sunday, and the ships based in Honolulu were always in port on Saturday and Sunday. It would take almost two weeks for his task force to reach Hawaii and for an invasion force to reach Malaya. That meant the ships would have to leave Japan on November 25—before the deadline for negotiations. But they could be called back in the unlikely event Ambassador Nomura met with success. On November 25, the two forces sailed from Japan.

The fleet headed for Pearl Harbor had assembled in the Kurile Islands, their radios silenced. Their route to Hawaii was chosen to keep them away from shipping lanes, and outside the range of American patrol planes. The fleet sailing for Southeast Asia, on the other hand, was reported to Washington by American intelligence on the same day it left Japan. The room for diplomatic negotiation dwindled to zero. Secretary Hull immediately sent to Tokyo a list of ten conditions to be met before discussions could continue.

On December 1, the Japanese leaders reviewed Secretary Hull's ten points, rejected them all, and decided to go ahead with the attack. They prepared a message for Washington announcing Japan was breaking off the negotiations with the United States—a message implying war was the next step. They started the message on its way. And they gave the orders for attacks: on Malaya, the British Island colony of Hong Kong just off the South China coast, the East Indies, the Philippines, the United States island bases of Guam, Midway, and Wake Islands, and on Pearl Harbor.

On December 7, as Admiral Yamamoto listened to radio reports of the damage inflicted at Pearl Harbor, he turned to one of his officers with a question. "The government's last declaration to the United States was scheduled to be delivered before our attack began," he said. "But I would like you to check it."

"I believe the note was delivered as scheduled," the officer replied.

"Nevertheless, I want you to check it."

In the next forty years many military courts would examine that question. Many historians would write books about it. Many aspects of the answer are still debated. For Admiral Yamamoto, delivery of the message meant that his surprise attack was within the accepted code of honor. It was the equivalent of a gunfighter in the Wild West calling to his opponent so that he could turn and face him and perhaps draw his gun. Without the message, the attack was the equivalent of a shot in the back.

In brief, the facts are that on December 6, the Japanese government sent the long message by radio, in code, to Ambassador Nomura. The accompanying instructions said he should have it typed and ready for delivery to Secretary of State Hull at a time to be set later. On Sunday morning, December 7, further instructions set the time of delivery at 1 P.M. that very day. There was not enough time to comply, and Ambassador Nomura reached the State Department at 2:05. Between 1:00 and 2:00, the first bombs fell at Pearl Harbor, where, because of the difference in time zones, it was still early Sunday morning. It had been decided on December 1 to send the message. It is still debated whether the long delay was intentional or simply the result of bureaucratic slowness.

To complicate further the answer to the question, United States intelligence had decoded the two messages as usual, and copies of them were circulating around Washington, where everyone agreed that Japan's breaking off negotiations meant war in the Pacific. But few believed Japan would declare war on the United States, and of that few almost nobody expected the war to begin nearly four thousand miles from Japan, at Pearl Harbor.

These subtle considerations were raised much later. On

December 8, President Roosevelt spoke to the United States Congress. He called December 7 "a day that will live in infamy," and the American people agreed. He asked the Congress to declare "that a state of war exists between Japan and the United States," and the Congress quickly did so. The war had become the Second World War.

In Tokyo the high command were elated. Admiral Yamamoto's surprise attack had won a major victory, as he had predicted. Eight American battleships, three cruisers and three destroyers were damaged in the attack. Two of the battleships, the *Arizona* and the *Oklahoma*, would never fight again. American aircraft losses were also heavy: ninety-two planes of the navy and ninety-six of the army air corps. The navy suffered by far the heaviest loss of men, 2008 killed and 710 wounded. Japan lost no ships in the attack, and only twenty-nine out of 353 planes. The only item in the battle report to cause major regret in Tokyo concerned the two United States aircraft carriers based at Pearl Harbor. Neither one had come into port that weekend, as the Japanese had expected them to, and therefore both had escaped damage.

While Pearl Harbor was Japan's most important victory, the rest of the December 7 attacks went well, too. Bombers based in Taiwan attacked two airfields near Manila in the Philippines and found all the American planes on the ground. They destroyed all eighteen of the Flying Fortress bombers (the B-17s), and fifty-three P-40 fighter planes.

Within days, invasion forces in overwhelming numbers approached Malaya, Hong Kong, Guam, and Wake. On Wake Island five hundred defenders, mostly United States Marines, managed to inflict such heavy losses on the Japanese that they withdrew to await reinforcements. But by the end of December, Wake, Guam, and Hong Kong had all been overcome.

Singapore was often referred to as "Britain's impregnable fortress in the Far East." The description was accurate insofar as Singapore was a naval base, impossible to overcome by *naval* attack. The British considered it adequately protected from land attack by the tropical jungle to its north. But they had not taken into consideration the rigorous training of the Japanese foot soldiers, which had toughened them to endure enormous hardships; or the zeal of their fighting for their emperor. A Japanese fleet landed an invasion force well north of Singapore, which captured all the British airfields in northern Malaya. Britain's two largest warships in the Orient, the new battleship *Prince of Wales* and the battle cruiser *Repulse*, left Singapore to meet the enemy fleet. They discovered another factor they had not taken into consideration in their planning—the vulnerability of even the mightiest battleships to bombs and torpedoes dropped from airplanes. The sudden loss of the airfields deprived the British ships of any aerial protection. Their own guns were inadequate to deal with the waves of Japanese navy planes that attacked them, and both ships were sunk. By December 11, Japan controlled both sea and air north of Singapore. Japanese armies fought south through Malaya, and on January 31, laid siege to the impregnable fortress itself. The defenders, their water supply destroyed by bombing and shelling, with no hope of help arriving by sea, surrendered on Friday the thirteenth of February. The loss of the two great ships and of the base was a heavy blow to morale in Britain and in the United States.

Another "impregnable fortress" remained, in the Philippines: Corregidor Island, a fortified "rock" at the entrance to Manila Bay. Commanding in the Philippines was one of America's best military strategists, General Douglas MacArthur. On December 22, a Japanese invasion force landed north of Manila, and a second soon followed, south of the city. MacArthur, recognizing it was impossible to defend Manila, decided to assemble all his forces in the peninsula opposite Corregidor, to protect the island and control sea access to the city. The name of the peninsula, Bataan, and the name Corregidor soon appeared every day in the newspapers in the United States, along with the name of MacArthur. "General Mac" and his American soldiers would show "those

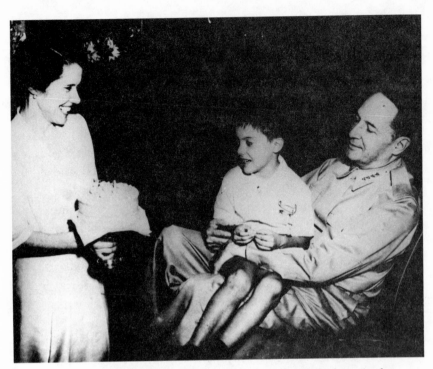

General Douglas MacArthur was commander of U.S. forces in the Philippine Islands when the Japanese attacked. He and his wife Jean celebrated the fourth birthday of their son Arthur, February 21, 1942, in the island fortress of Corregidor—"The Rock." The next month the three MacArthurs traveled to Australia in a small patrol torpedo boat in order for the general to accept command of the counteroffensive.

Japs" what fighting was all about, editors wrote. MacArthur knew how desperate the situation was, unless more men and more airplanes could be supplied him, but he intended at least to show the Japanese what courage was all about. He intended to hold out on Corregidor until reinforcements arrived or he himself was killed or captured. In the meantime, he spoke stirring words to his men, which were reported in full back in the United States, and helped to rouse the American people to action after the shock of Pearl Harbor.

President Roosevelt could not risk sending reinforcements through seas where the Japanese navy was likely to wipe them out before they ever got a chance to fight. But MacArthur was needed to plan and command the whole Pacific war. Therefore President Roosevelt sent a personal message to MacArthur ordering him to go to Australia to begin planning a counteroffensive against the Japanese, as commander of all American forces in the southwest Pacific. After days of delay, MacArthur agreed. He and his wife and their four-year-old son left Corregidor at night on March 11 in a small patrol torpedo boat, for a rendezvous with a plane that took them to Australia. There he spoke the words that became a slogan for the counteroffensive: "I shall return."

In April, the Japanese increased their air attacks on the men on Bataan, already suffering from hunger, many of them feverish with malaria, with no new supplies of food or medicine in prospect. They surrendered. In May the men on Corregidor had to do the same.

Even before Singapore and the Philippines fell, the Japanese proceeded to their most important objective: the Dutch East Indies oil. They took the islands one by one, until they came at last to Java, where the headquarters of the Allied forces was located. A naval force made up of Dutch, British, Australian, and United States ships, including five cruisers, went out to meet the invasion fleet in the Java Sea, but the Allies had no aircraft to fly reconnaissance. The Japanese suffered some losses, but sank all five of the Allied cruisers. They then landed their troops and took Java, just three months after Pearl Harbor. The seizure of the European colonies had run well ahead of schedule and seemed a marvelous success.

10
Counterattack

In April, 1942, Japan's newly conquered empire stretched from Malaya on the continent of Asia eastward to Guam and Wake Island in the Pacific, and south to the Dutch East Indies. According to the plan of the Japanese high command, it was time to forge around this empire the "ring of steel" composed of Admiral Yamamoto's ships. They would protect it while the Japanese used its rich resources to give their military machine the supplies needed to complete the conquest of China. Once that was done, all the nations in the area, under Japan's leadership, could develop as part of a "Greater East Asia Co-prosperity Sphere." Soon their former masters, the European colonial powers and the United States of America, the plan continued, would recognize Japan's invincibility. They called themselves "Allies" against the Axis powers. But tired of war, those "Allies" would ask to negotiate a peace in the Pacific. Japan's victory would be complete. She would be, at last, master of Asia.

Two major islands in the western Pacific remained in Allied hands: the island continent of Australia, and the fifteen-hundred-mile-long island of New Guinea, just off Australia's northern tip. If the naval "ring of steel" was to be complete, New Guinea must be conquered also, and Australia either conquered or blockaded so that she could not participate effectively in the war. After conquering the Dutch East Indies, then, the Japanese moved right ahead to attack New Guinea. There the Japanese plan of conquest bogged down for the first time.

In May, 1942, Admiral Yamamoto sent three aircraft carriers and other ships to attack a major Allied base on the southeast tip of New Guinea. Before his ships got to their target, they encountered for the first time a force directed by Admiral Yamamoto's counterpart in the United States Navy, Admiral Chester W. Nimitz. Admiral Nimitz had been named Commander in Chief of the United States Pacific Fleet on December 31 and had been calmly planning how best to respond to Japan's actions. It took several months to assemble enough ships to challenge Japanese might, but now he was ready.

Off New Guinea, in the Coral Sea, two American task forces intercepted the Japanese. Key ships were the two American aircraft carriers that had luckily been away from their Pearl Harbor base on December 7: the *Enterprise* and the *Lexington*. With them now were two other carriers, the *Yorktown* and the *Hornet*. For the first time in history, a major naval battle took place without the ships ever coming in sight of each other. Planes from the carriers did all the damage. The Japanese sank the carrier *Lexington*. The Americans sank the Japanese carrier *Shoho* and put the other two out of action for some weeks. The battle of the Coral Sea, May 4–8, 1942, cannot be counted a victory for either side, but it stopped the steady Japanese advance. From then on, victory was not to be so easy as the Japanese high command had thought.

Another event just three weeks earlier had also dented

Japanese confidence—and again an American aircraft carrier was responsible. The airplanes of early 1942 all had a limited range. Carrier-based planes could fly a few hundred miles before they ran out of fuel. Larger land-based bombers could fly perhaps fifteen hundred miles. The Japanese were sure that their island home was well beyond the range of possible aerial attack. Yet on April 18, sixteen American B-25 bombers appeared in the sky over Tokyo and dropped their bombs. Where had they come from? Where was the "ring of steel"?

The answer, the Japanese learned later, was that a group of Army Air Force pilots, led by Lieutenant Colonel Jimmy Doolittle, had learned how to take off in the heavy B-25s from the deck of an aircraft carrier. The carrier *Hornet* had brought them within seven hundred miles of Japan, they had taken off, bombed Tokyo, and then continued on to friendly airfields—or crash landings—in China and Russia. They were some of the first American heroes of the war, and Colonel Doolittle's picture was hung in schoolrooms across the United States.

Looking back, some of the basic elements in the Allied war effort can be seen in the Battle of the Coral Sea and the Tokyo air raid. For fighting, the aircraft carrier had replaced the battleship as the foundation for naval strategy. The army, navy and air force of each Allied nation cooperated closely in overall planning, and also cooperated with the forces of the other nations. And at the highest level, the heads of state conferred and set priorities in the war. British Prime Minister Winston Churchill had visited President Franklin Roosevelt in Washington in December, soon after Japan's Axis partners, Germany and Italy, had declared war on the United States. Roosevelt and Churchill had decided to concentrate on defeating Germany first, before giving their full attention to defeating Japan. But Roosevelt was also in constant touch with Chiang Kai-shek and was trying to get the Russians to allow supplies for China to be transported across Russian territory. Australian, Canadian, Dutch, French, and other

Aircraft carriers played a major role in the war in the Pacific. On April 18, 1942, Lt. Col. Jimmy Doolittle's squadron of B-25 bombers, normally based on land, took off from the flight deck of the USS Hornet to deliver a surprise attack on Tokyo.

leaders were also consulted, and their armed forces included in war plans.

A really keen Japanese observer might have noticed other aspects of the Allied war effort, less specific but important to the final outcome. There was a willingness, even an eagerness, to try new ways of fighting, abandoning the accepted wisdom of the military colleges. That extended to the development of a whole arsenal of new weapons, using Western technology and industrial skills. Then there was an eloquence in the speeches of the leaders, especially Roosevelt and Churchill, that rallied ordinary citizens behind the war and made them feel that their duty to their countries was every bit as holy as the Japanese citizens' duty to their emperor. In particular the attack on Pearl Harbor had made the Americans fighting mad, after years of attempting to live in isolation from the world. And there was bravery, as shown by Colonel Doolittle's pilots, equal to that of any samurai.

The Japanese war effort was much less coordinated. The navy and the army were always jealous of each other, and each refused to take direction from the other. And Japan's supposed partners, Germany and Italy, made no contributions to the war in the Pacific. Hitler had not advised the Japanese before he invaded Russia in June 1941, although Russia's long border with China and Manchuria made Japan intensely concerned with what happened in Russia. Japan, of course, had told no one about the plan to attack Pearl Harbor, although it was sure to bring the United States into the war against the Axis powers.

After the Battle of the Coral Sea thwarted the naval attack on New Guinea, the Japanese high command decided to land troops and fight overland to the Allied base there, as they had fought overland in Malaya to Singapore. These landings gained toeholds on the island. But the terrain of New Guinea was even more hostile than the jungles of Malaya. Mountains rose over ten thousand feet. Swamps and forests blocked the way. And in the forests lived tribes who had never seen foreigners before, but who practiced headhunting among those they considered their enemies. Advances were slow, to say the least. It seemed the "ring of steel" would take longer to complete than expected.

At that point Admiral Yamamoto decided to speed up a few parts of the long-range plan. The United States Pacific Fleet, despite its losses at Pearl Harbor, was obviously still strong enough to give him trouble. He did not intend to allow another desecration of the sacred soil of Japan like the bombing attack on Tokyo. He would send ships in overwhelming numbers to engage the American fleet and destroy it completely.

His only problem, as he saw it, was to ensure that the

engagement took place where he wanted it to. That fleet was based in Pearl Harbor still. If the engagement occurred close to Hawaii, the American fleet would have the advantage of land-based aerial support from the airfields there. He must lure it away. The most likely way, he believed, was to attack the one small island that the Allies still held between Hawaii and Japan: Midway Island. At the same time he would attack the Aleutian Island chain jutting far out across the Pacific from Alaska. The Americans would then divide their ships to protect both Midway and Alaska, and he would annihilate them all.

Admiral Yamamoto was right that the Americans would send some ships to Alaska and some to Midway. But he was wrong to think they would do that only after he attacked. He was wrong because he did not know the most important fact in the whole situation: American intelligence was reporting all his plans to Admiral Nimitz, as a result of having broken the code the Japanese navy used for radio messages. When the lead ships of his huge fleet reached Midway, the Americans were waiting for them. This time, surprise was on the side of the Americans. The nastiest surprise for Yamamoto was the presence of those three carriers *Yorktown*, *Enterprise*, and *Hornet* that had done him so much damage in the Battle of the Coral Sea.

Admiral Nimitz's plan was simple: while the planes from Japanese carriers attacked Midway, planes from American carriers would attack the Japanese carriers. At dawn on June 4, 1942, the Japanese planes took off. Less than two hours later the Americans took off, and by midmorning three Japanese carriers were in flames. Explosions of their own stocks of bombs, torpedoes, and aviation gasoline completed their destruction. By sunset, a fourth Japanese carrier and a cruiser had been fatally hit. Japanese pilots had found one of the American carriers, the *Yorktown* and scored two torpedo hits. That had not been enough to sink that often-damaged, often-repaired veteran, but while she was being towed from the

battle by a destroyer, a Japanese submarine sank both her
and the destroyer.

The Battle of Midway cost the Americans one carrier and
one destroyer, 150 planes and 307 lives. It cost the Japanese
four carriers, one cruiser, 322 planes and thirty-five hundred
men. Early on the morning of June 5, Admiral Yamamoto
ordered his fleet to turn back toward Japan. The Allies had
won their first victory in the Pacific. It was small consolation
to the Japanese that on June 7 the attackers captured the
small islands of Kiska and Attu, at the tip of the Aleutian
chain.

All through the summer of 1942 the Japanese army continued
fighting its way across New Guinea. After the rapid conquest
of so many countries, the high command expanded its ambitions to include the conquest of Australia. New Britain
and the Solomon Islands, northeast of Australia, had fallen
easily, and the Japanese had developed a great air and sea base
at Rabaul on New Britain. But New Guinea had not fallen,
and its Allied base, at Port Moresby, balanced the Japanese
base at Rabaul.

General MacArthur resolved to defend Port Moresby with
all vigor. Allied resistance, combined with the terrible terrain, slowed the Japanese advance so much that in September,
thirty-two miles from the prize, the army ran out of food and
had to turn back.

On August 7, eight months after Pearl Harbor, the Allies
were ready for their first counteroffensive in the Pacific. The
long-term goal, of course, was to hand Japan so many defeats
that she would have to give up the territory she had conquered. General MacArthur was assigned the Southwest Pacific Area Command, based in Australia. Admiral Nimitz
was assigned the Pacific Ocean Areas Command, based in
Hawaii.

The Allied counteroffensive began at the southeast corner
of Japan's new empire, with one of the islands most recently
conquered, Guadalcanal in the Solomon Islands. Guadal-

canal, once retaken, could provide airfields for attacks on the Japanese base at Rabaul. The United States Marine Corps, whose members prided themselves on being America's toughest fighters, was given the assignment of this first counterattack. The Japanese resisted fiercely, with even the youngest soldiers remembering the samurai motto "Death before dishonor." It was the following February before the Marines, reinforced by units of the United States Army, ended the last resistance on Guadalcanal.

Admiral Yamamoto was on the scene in the Solomon Islands, directing naval operations. On April 14, 1943, American intelligence heard a radio message that he would fly to Bougainville Island on April 18, arriving about 9:30 in the morning. Bougainville was within range of American P-38 fighter planes taking off from Guadalcanal, but just barely. On April 18, sixteen P38s flew to Bougainville, hoping the admiral would arrive before their fuel supplies forced them to return to base. Admiral Yamamoto practiced the punctuality of the career naval officer. At 9:35, P-38 pilot Lieutenant Thomas Lanphier shot off the left wing of the Admiral's plane. It crashed in the jungle, killing one of the best strategists Japan had.

Rabaul on New Britain was much more strongly defended than Guadalcanal. When one of his officers asked MacArthur how he would ever take such strongpoints, he replied, "I don't want them." What the Allies did want was control of the air and the sea. If they achieved that, they could cut off supplies to all the Japanese forces, and eventually supplies to Japan herself. The Battle of Midway had gone a long way toward giving the Allies control of the sea. To gain control of the air, MacArthur and Nimitz planned to attack small, less strongly defended islands and build airfields on them. They simply went around the Japanese strongpoints. "Islandhopping" the press called it. "Leapfrogging" was MacArthur's name for it.

The Japanese saw what the enemy was doing, but found

no effective countermeasures. In the vast distances of the Pacific—a battleground whose dimensions they had set themselves—they could not guess where the Allies would strike next. They only knew that each strike would be a little closer to Japan's home islands. And the immense resources of the United States, which Admiral Yamamoto had warned about in 1940, were beginning to tell. American factories were turning out more and more ships and planes, and the planes were getting bigger and bigger, with longer and longer ranges. It seemed inevitable that one day bombers could fly from some newly recaptured island to Tokyo itself.

There was another Allied tactic that made it difficult for the Japanese high command to make the orderly battle plans they excelled in: the use of submarines. Germany had perfected that type of warfare in the North Atlantic. The Allies had learned there to group their ships, including their merchant ships, in convoys, protected by fast destroyers. And they had learned to use submarines themselves. Now Allied submarines were roaming the waters inside the naval "ring of steel," most of which still existed only on the high command's planning board. The submarines were almost impossible to spot as long as they stayed underwater, and when they were "hunting," their crews would go for incredibly long periods without coming up. They were sinking the merchant ships that were supposed to be bringing home the oil and other resources of the conquered territories for the use of Japan's armed forces. Often the captain of an Allied sub "got lucky" and sank a ship of the Japanese navy.

The list of islands captured after Guadalcanal is a long one, including Bougainville, Tarawa, Kwajalein, Hollandia, Guam, Saipan and Peleliu. They are tiny specks barely visible on the map, but big enough to serve either Japan or the Allies as "unsinkable aircraft carriers." On every one of them Japanese troops fought grimly to the end, with no thought of surrender. Saipan was close enough to Japan for the new B-29 superfortress bombers to bomb Tokyo, not just once as

U.S. Marines fighting to take the island of Tarawa in the South Pacific, as part of General MacArthur's "leapfrog" strategy. Each island captured from Japan served as an air base for attacks that advanced ever closer to Tokyo.

Colonel Doolittle and his men had done, but time after time. Prime Minister Tojo, who was also Minister of War Tojo, knew that, and resigned his posts when Saipan fell.

Peleliu was only four hundred miles from the Philippines. No one had forgotten General MacArthur's promise, "I shall return." On October 20, 1944, United States units, supported by ships and airplanes, landed on the island of Leyte, in the central Philippines. Five hours after the first landing, General MacArthur, sixty-four years old, waded ashore.

Allied naval strength in the Pacific had grown to the point where 218 American ships, belonging to the Third and the Seventh Fleets, were covering the Leyte operation. The Japanese resolved to fall upon them in Leyte Gulf, hoping to destroy them, and stop the invasion. They sent fleets from north and south, all the strength the Imperial Navy had left, to accomplish this. Included was the superbattleship *Musashi*. (The *Musashi* and its twin the *Yamato* were the largest battleships ever built—sixty-nine thousand tons each.) In tonnage of ships involved on the two sides, it was the greatest naval engagement in history.

Although it is called the Battle of Leyte Gulf, the battle actually took place in waters all around Leyte, with the opposing fleets playing a sort of deadly hide and seek among small islands and racing to block narrow straits at either end of Leyte. On October 23, three days after General MacArthur waded ashore, one Japanese fleet sent from the south arrived just west of Leyte. That day American submarines sank two of its cruisers. The next day, planes from the United States Third Fleet attacked and sank the *Musashi*. Then they spotted a fleet sent from the north, and the Third Fleet went to meet it, as the Japanese hoped it would. That left the strait north of Leyte open, and the fleet from the south dashed through to attack the United States Seventh Fleet. The Seventh Fleet urgently requested the Third Fleet to come back. The Seventh Fleet's men fought bravely and successfully against great odds, until the Japanese commander, fearing the Third Fleet would cut off the strait that was his escape route, broke off the battle and went back the way he had come. Another Japanese fleet from the south had even less success. As it entered the strait south of Leyte, it found the way blocked by an American task force, which quickly sank two Japanese battleships and four destroyers.

On the third day of the battle, things were going so badly for the Japanese that their carrier pilots tried a new solution to a problem of their profession: on any mission, many planes

Young Japanese pilots preparing for a suicide raid on Allied warships.
They tried to crash their planes onto their targets, ensuring a direct hit and
a hero's death. The Japanese gave them the name Kamikaze, divine winds,
after a typhoon that saved Japan from a Mongol invasion in 1281.

used up precious oil, bombs, and torpedoes to attack a target—
and missed. That day, the pilots began to crash their planes
onto their targets. That greatly improved their chances of a
direct hit—and of dying a hero's death for the emperor. The
American sailors called them "suicide squads." But the Japanese had a more poetic name: *kamikaze*, "divine winds," in
memory of a typhoon that had saved Japan from an invasion
by the Mongols in the year 1281.

There was no salvation for the Japanese at Leyte Gulf.
They lost the *Musashi* and two other battleships, four carriers, ten cruisers, and nine destroyers. The Americans lost
one light carrier, two escort carriers, two destroyers, and one
destroyer escort. The strength of the Imperial Fleet, weakened
at Midway, was now almost entirely gone.

The invasion of Leyte continued. In December it fell to
the Americans. In January 1945, United States forces landed
on the island of Luzon and began the fight for Manila. With
the Allies now in control of the seas, it was impossible for the

Japanese to send supplies and reinforcements there, but the sons of the samurai fought on with what supplies they had, augmented by courage and a firm belief in the way of the warrior. It was the same on every island the Allies invaded: Iwo Jima in February and Okinawa in April. On Iwo Jima twenty-three thousand Japanese fought for a month, until the last man was dead, and twenty thousand Americans were dead or wounded. The battle for Okinawa lasted ten weeks, resulted in one hundred and nine thousand Japanese deaths and produced forty-nine thousand Allied casualties. The Allies were getting closer to the home islands of Japan, but the Japanese were making them pay a heavy price for every gain.

In Tokyo, the Emperor Hirohito read the casualty figures with a heavy heart. He had realized in the first year after Pearl Harbor that it had been a mistake to believe the boasts of his military leaders and to give his authorization for the 1941 plan of conquest. Now, in addition to the losses of soldiers and sailors and airmen, he must bear responsibility for the deaths of thousands of Japanese civilians. The tactic of bombing cities, which the Japanese had used with small planes at Shanghai in 1936, had been expanded by the Germans in Europe in 1939 and 1940. Now the Allies were using it daily against Japan. First there had been occasional raids by planes based in southwest China. The high command had ordered the troops there into action again in 1944, and they had taken most of the Allied airfields. They had also attempted an invasion of northeast India to take the airfields there. That invasion had failed, and now the Allies were regaining most of the airfields in southwest China. But they did not really need them. Now they had Saipan. As expected, bombers based there were now bombing Tokyo and other major Japanese cities. Fires caused by the bombs had swept through the cities, leaving as much as forty percent of them in ruins.

The emperor's loyal subjects bore all this—loss of their loved ones, loss of their homes and businesses, loss of their pride in their country's invincible might—with a listlessness that was frightening. Hirohito knew they were hungry. Japan had not raised enough food for its population since the nineteenth century, and now three-quarters of its merchant ships were sunk. There was no way to bring in enough food to feed the people.

April, 1945, brought Japan a number of unhappy events, beginning with the Allied invasion of Okinawa. The prime minister who had followed General Tojo resigned in his turn and was replaced by Admiral Suzuki Kantaro. The new prime minister wanted to end the war, but he believed that if the Japanese could win at least one battle on Okinawa, the Allies would agree to easier terms for peace. At his orders, the fighting and dying on Okinawa continued. The Soviet Union gave Japan a year's notice that the Soviet-Japanese Neutrality Pact, due to expire in April, 1946, would not be renewed. The Japanese did not know that in February, 1945, the Soviet Premier Joseph Stalin had promised Roosevelt and Churchill that the Soviet Union would enter the war against Japan two or three months after Germany surrendered. That surrender seemed not far away, for Allied armies were pushing across Germany from both east and west. Soviet troops entered the suburbs of Berlin on April 22. Germany surrendered two weeks later. The Axis alliance was no more. Japan was left to fight the full might of the Allied nations alone.

Also in April, President Franklin Roosevelt died and was succeeded by President Harry Truman.

By June 1945, Japan's stock of oil was so low that the government tried to barter some navy cruisers to the Soviet Union for oil. When this did not work, the military high command admitted there was no way to continue the war, and in July the government asked the Soviet Union to act as mediator for peace negotiations. The reply was that Stalin, Churchill, and Truman were about to meet at the town of Potsdam in Germany to discuss the future, and nothing could be done until after that meeting.

The meeting produced, on July 26, the joint Potsdam Declaration, of the United States and Great Britain, with Stalin and Chiang Kai-shek concurring. It called on Japan to end the war. It promised that Japan would continue as a nation, limited to the "home islands"—her territory before her conquests. Japan would be governed for a time by an army of occupation, until a peacefully inclined and responsible government had been established "in accordance with the freely expressed will of the Japanese people." The final paragraph read: "We call upon the government of Japan to proclaim now the unconditional surrender of all Japanese armed forces and to provide proper and adequate assurances of their good faith in such action. The alternative for Japan is prompt and utter destruction."

In July only a few people in the world knew the full significance of the declaration's words "utter destruction." To the Japanese high command it meant a continuation of the bombing of Japanese cities and after that an invasion of the home islands. If the sons of the samurai had made the Allies pay dearly for every scrap of island they had invaded, what price would the entire population of the nation exact for the sacred soil of Japan? There followed days of discussion in Tokyo. Would continued Allied losses, intensified as the fighting reached the home islands, produce some lessening of the demand for *unconditional* surrender? There was one condition everyone felt was absolutely essential: the monarchy, which had ruled Japan in an unbroken line through one hundred twenty-four emperors, must continue. If the Allies would agree to that condition—and the Potsdam Declaration said nothing about the monarchy one way or the other—then the war could end. If not, some felt the war must go on.

The emperor himself wanted to spare his people further suffering. But he had been taught as a boy that it was not the emperor's place to decide national policy. That was the responsibility of the ministers of the government. He listened gravely to reports of their discussions. On July 28, Prime Minister Suzuki held a press conference in which he spoke of the Potsdam Declaration in a rather ambiguous way. The Allies interpreted his words to mean Japan rejected their terms.

By August 6, the discussions whether to continue the war had still reached no conclusion. That day utter destruction visited the city of Hiroshima, five hundred fifty miles south of Tokyo. The American bomber *Enola Gay* dropped the world's first atomic bomb. It completely destroyed the city, killed ninety-two thousand people, and released radiation that caused thousands more to die horribly in the weeks and years to come. President Truman announced to the world: "It was to spare the Japanese from utter destruction that the ultimatum of July 26 was issued at Potsdam. Their leaders promptly rejected that ultimatum. If they do not now accept our terms they may expect a rain of ruin from the air, the like of which has never been seen on this earth."

The foreign minister went to see Emperor Hirohito the next day and told him that he believed the unprecedented devastation at Hiroshima gave an opportunity to end the war, despite the fact that the minister of war and other military men still favored fighting on. The Emperor agreed: "We must not let this opportunity slip away. And we must not waste it in attempts to gain more favorable conditions." He sent word of his opinion to Prime Minister Suzuki.

At eleven o'clock that night, Tokyo time, Soviet Foreign Minister Vyacheslav Molotov told the Japanese ambassador in Moscow that the Soviet Union would declare war on Japan the next day, August 9. On that day Soviet troops moved across the border into Manchuria. And the prime minister, Admiral Suzuki, went to see the emperor. He told him that he had now made up his mind that Japan must accept the Potsdam demands. Then, in the face of unprecedented di-

In July 26, 1945, the Allies warned the Japanese that they must surrender or face "utter destruction." On August 6 the U.S. dropped the first atomic bomb on the city of Hiroshima (above). The blast killed 92,000 people, and thousands more died of radiation sickness in the weeks and years that followed.

saster, he made an unprecedented request: he asked the emperor to assist him in securing the agreement of the army men in the high command. "Of course I'll give you my assistance," Hirohito said.

As Prime Minister Suzuki expected, the meeting of the Supreme Council for the Direction of the War that same morning resulted in a deadlock. Then news arrived that an American plane had dropped a second atomic bomb, this time on the great port of Nagasaki on the west coast of the island of Kyushu. The meeting broke up with no decision reached. The Cabinet of Ministers met that afternoon, and still the minister of war prevented a decision for peace. Prime Minister Suzuki then called for an "Imperial Conference"—a joint meeting of the Supreme Council and the Cabinet of Ministers, held in the presence of the emperor.

The Imperial Conference began at 11:30 that night, in the emperor's personal air raid shelter, sixty feet underground beneath the gardens of his palace. For two hours those present gave their conflicting opinions. Prime Minister Suzuki summarized; then he bowed and spoke these startling words: "I present myself humbly at the foot of the throne, and I request your Imperial Majesty's opinion . . . . "

Hirohito was one of the few in the room prepared for that request. He rose and made what was for him a long speech, of several paragraphs. He went over the current desperate military situation of Japan and expressed his sadness at what lay ahead. "Nevertheless," he concluded, "the time has come when we must bear the unbearable. When I think of the feelings of my Imperial Grandsire, the Emperor Meiji, at the time of the Triple Intervention [of 1895] I swallow my own tears and give my sanction to the proposal to accept the Allied proclamation on the basis outlined by the foreign minister."

At 6:00 A.M., August 10, the foreign minister sent a note to the United States, Great Britain, China, and the Soviet Union saying that Japan accepted the Potsdam Declaration, so long as it did not prejudice the prerogatives of the emperor as a sovereign ruler. Two days later the United States secretary of state replied that the form of government of Japan would be determined by "the freely expressed will of the Japanese people." That produced two more days of debate in the Supreme Council and the Cabinet of Ministers.

Meanwhile, word spread of the possibility that the government would admit that Japan was defeated, for the first time in her long history. Certain army officers decided that they were seeing a repetition of a situation that had occurred several times in the nation's history: the emperor had received bad advice from his ministers and must be rescued from their evil influence. They proposed to the minister of war a military takeover of the nation, beginning with a takeover of the imperial palace. The minister refused to go along with that plan, and the officers then turned to recruiting members of the emperor's palace guard to help them.

On the morning of August 14, Hirohito took the initiative in calling another Imperial Conference. He acknowledged that the Japanese people would be deeply shocked when they heard of this decision. "If it is considered appropriate," he said, "I am willing to go on the radio and explain the matter to them personally." The people had never heard the emperor's voice. The broadcast would be an event in itself. Hirohito also acknowledged that the minister of war and the navy minister might have difficulty persuading their men to accept the decision to surrender. He offered to go wherever necessary to explain the decision to them.

"I now request the cabinet, therefore," he said, "to prepare at once an imperial rescript [order] which I shall broadcast to the nation, announcing the termination of the war." That night he made a recording of the message, to be broadcast at noon the next day.

During the night the palace grounds were the scene of a real-life drama equal to any samurai thriller. An army major, the leader of the conspiracy to prevent the surrender, visited the commander of the palace guards and invited him to join in saving Japan from disgrace. The commander replied that before he could make such a decision he would have to go to the shrine of the Emperor Meiji to pray. Soon the major knew time was running out; he shot the commander and forged his name on orders to the guards to seal off the palace grounds. He hoped that much of the army would support his plan for a military takeover, once he had the emperor safely in custody. His men searched the buildings on the palace grounds for advisors known to favor peace, but since they knew neither the buildings nor the faces of the men they were looking for, the search failed. Some of their intended victims escaped through secret passageways built centuries before. Others simply bluffed their way through encounters with the conspirators, realizing they were not recognized. A frantic search for the recording of the emperor's message to the people also failed—it was locked in a safe hidden by stacks of old documents. In Tokyo, other conspirators went looking for Prime Minister Suzuki to assassinate him, but he and his family were warned in time to leave their home.

At 5:00 A.M. the general commanding the army responsible for the defense of Tokyo arrived at the palace grounds. He told the guards they were acting on forged orders and sent them back to their barracks. The leader of the conspiracy, realizing the army would not rally behind him, committed suicide.

All that morning of August 15, every radio station in Japan announced that the emperor would speak to the nation at noon. Only a few men knew what he would say. Many Japanese put on formal dress to hear the voice of their divine ruler. At noon an announcer asked the nation to stand for a broadcast "of the highest importance." The national anthem followed, and then the high-pitched voice of Hirohito. He announced that he had ordered the government to communicate acceptance of the Potsdam Declaration. He summarized the aims of the war, and said, in a sentence carefully phrased to spare the pride of the military, that the war situation had "developed not necessarily to Japan's advantage." He mentioned the new kind of bomb used by the enemy. "Should we continue to fight, it would not only result in an ultimate collapse and obliteration of the Japanese nation, but also it would lead to the total extinction of human civilization. Such being the case, how are We to save the millions of our subjects; or to atone Ourselves before the hallowed spirits of Our Imperial Ancestors? This is the reason why We have ordered the acceptance . . . . We have resolved to pave the way to peace for ten thousand generations by enduring the unendurable and suffering what is insufferable." He asked his people to beware of "outbursts of emotion which may engender needless complications, or any fraternal contention and strife which may create confusion." He concluded with a call to unite and work with resolution to build the future of Japan.

So ended the most far-reaching plan of conquest of modern times.

I I

Rebuilding
a Nation

 At the end of August, 1945, two weeks after
Emperor Hirohito announced to his people
that their government had accepted the surrender terms of the Allied nations, the military
occupation of Japan began. It lasted for almost
seven years. In that time, between victor and vanquished there
developed a relationship unlike any ever before in the history
of war. The occupation had profound effects on both the
Japanese and the Allies.

The formal surrender document was signed on September 2 aboard the American battleship *Missouri*, anchored in
Tokyo Bay. Foreign Minister Shigemitsu Mamoru and General Umeza Yoshijiro signed for Japan. Supreme Commander
of the Allied Powers General Douglas MacArthur signed for
the Allies, and Admiral Chester Nimitz for the United States
of America. At that time Japan's armies were still in place in
the territory they had conquered on the continent of Asia.

The formal document of Japanese surrender was signed on September 2, 1945, on board the battleship USS Missouri by representatives of Japan and of the Allies. Admiral Chester Nimitz signs for the U.S.

Those in China were directed to surrender to Chiang Kai-shek. Those in Japan and in Korea south of the 38th parallel of latitude were directed to surrender to General MacArthur. Those in the northern half of Korea and in Manchuria were to surrender to the commander of the forces of the newest participant in the Pacific War, the Soviet Union. China, the United States and the Soviet Union were Allies in the war. But these specific surrender details had profound effects on the areas involved.

The military occupation of Japan was officially an Allied effort. But only the United States had the manpower available for occupation duty. The British Commonwealth of Nations sent a few units. The other Allies sent representatives to the international councils that were charged with setting policy. In reality, the Supreme Commander of the Allied Powers, General Douglas MacArthur, made most of the decisions. Thus the occupation was basically American.

Americans had given much thought to the questions of why they were fighting World War II and what sort of a world they could expect when it was over. The World War of 1914–1918 had been described to them as "the war to end all wars." The destruction of World War II was much greater. They wanted to identify and avoid the mistakes made after 1918. They wanted to build from the wartime partnership of the Allied nations a peacetime organization much more effective than the old League of Nations.

But there was disagreement over what mistakes had been made before in the treatment of conquered Germany. Had she been treated too kindly, being left with the strength to wage another war in just twenty years? If so, Germany along with Japan, her partner, should now be reduced to simple farming nations, without industry of any sort. Or had Germany been treated too harshly after World War I, subjected to restrictions that made it impossible for her people to earn a good life for themselves by peaceful pursuits? If that was the mistake that led to World War II, then the Allies should help Germany and Japan to rebuild after the destruction of the war and help them at the same time to develop better forms of government. Whichever treatment was decided on, harsh or kind, everyone agreed Germany and Japan would not be allowed to maintain military forces.

After some debate at home, the Americans tended to favor the policy of helping the defeated nations rebuild, in order that they might participate in a healthy world economy. Since the Americans dominated the occupation of Japan, that was the kind of occupation they created there. Naturally there were some misgivings. Only a few months earlier, American patriotic speeches urging greater effort to win the war had described the Japanese as "fiendish." John Curtis Perry reports in his study of the occupation, *Beneath the Eagle's Wing*, that it was the children who "broke the ice." For example, a boatload of marines approached a naval base in Japan fingering their weapons. "Ten minutes after arriving on shore, the marines were giving chocolate bars to children." Immediately the Americans began building—one of their favorite activities.

There was much rebuilding to be done. The bombings had destroyed the homes of thirty percent of the people. Three-quarters of the nation's industry was out of action. Transportation and communication systems were barely functioning. And three million, one hundred thousand Japanese had lost their lives, including eight hundred thousand civilians. What had not been destroyed was the nation's capacity for hard work. When the Japanese saw that the occupation encouraged rebuilding, they gladly set to it with whatever tools and materials they could find. As for their attitude to the victors, a number of observers reported that the prevailing opinion seemed to be: "We lost. They won. Let's learn how they did it." The Japanese now call the period when their nation was controlled by its military men "The Dark Valley."

Hunger was the most pressing problem in the fall of 1945. Only the farmers had enough to eat. Japan had nothing like enough ships left to bring in food from abroad for her city dwellers. Women went out from the cities to farms every day to try to buy food for their families. Black markets developed, and inflation, so that Japanese money bought only one-hundredth of what it did before the war. How would Japan feed an army of occupation, when it could not feed itself? It came as a surprise that the Americans brought their own food with them, and plenty to spare. That was not the way conquering armies usually behaved. Day by day, the Japanese realized how unusual the American conquerers were.

Most unusual of all was General Douglas MacArthur.

William Manchester, biographer of several powerful world figures, called his life of MacArthur *American Caesar*. The General had a keen sense of history and his place in it and was fond of that sort of historical comparison. Like Commodore Perry, who arrived in Japan ninety-two years earlier, MacArthur had a flair for the dramatic, both in dress and in behavior. And like Perry, he had an instinctive sense that the quality that would win the respect of the Japanese was strength. As chief of the occupation, he was in fact the new ruler of Japan. He was a five-star general, the highest rank in the United States Army. But in the war he had another title that included a word the Japanese often used for top rank: "supreme." MacArthur was Supreme Commander for the Allied Powers, and that was the title he was known by in Japan. His official automobile had license plate number 1, with five stars. He set up his headquarters in a well-known Tokyo office building that had survived the bombings, the Dai Ichi Building—the name means "Number One." It is located directly opposite the imperial palace.

In that palace, Japan's hereditary ruler, the Emperor Hirohito, came to some conclusions about the future. He had called on his people to work for progress in his message announcing the surrender. Now he took some steps to set an example. On September 28, he sent word to MacArthur that he would like to speak with him. In other days, a foreigner in Japan would not be likely to see the emperor at all. If he was granted such an honor, he would go to an audience at the palace, dressed in special court clothes to show respect. MacArthur, of course, knew that and knew that a meeting must take place. He replied to Hirohito that his position would not allow him to come to the palace, and he did not expect the emperor to come to a public building, the Dai Ichi. He suggested the meeting take place at the American Embassy, not far away. They met there that same day.

Manchester quotes some words of Hirohito: "I come to you, General MacArthur, to offer myself to the judgment of

General MacArthur, as Supreme Commander of the Allied Powers, was in charge of the military occupation of Japan. On September 28, 1945, Emperor Hirohito and he met at the American Embassy, and both set to work rebuilding the future of the nation.

the powers you represent as the one to bear the sole responsibility for every . . . decision made and action taken by my people in the conduct of the war." MacArthur felt, he said afterwards, "moved . . . to the very marrow of my bones. He was an emperor by birth, but in that instant I knew I faced the First Gentleman of Japan in his own right."

For the meeting the emperor wore his formal tailcoat and striped trousers, now very old, and a silk top hat. MacArthur went directly from his office, in the immaculate khaki uniform, without necktie or medals, that was his everyday attire. The hat he wore was a personal trademark, a round khaki cap with a beak, crushed and casual looking, but trimmed with gold braid. The next day a photograph of the two men standing side by side appeared in papers all over Japan. The writer Hironaka Wakako, who was a student in the fifth grade at the time, says that photograph is one of the things she particularly remembers about that month. Seeing the contrast in the clothes of the two men, she knew that Japan was indeed defeated.

Hirohito began to set an example of work. This man of forty-four had rarely left the palace grounds except for a few ceremonial appearances. Now he began to tour Japan, to speak words of encouragement to his people and help their morale by his simple presence among them.

Despite the physical destruction of the war, the imperial government bureaucracy was still intact throughout the nation. The American occupation used that bureaucracy to run the day to day affairs of Japan. Otherwise, it would have been necessary to bring in many more men to set up an American military government, and the results would not have been as good. Japanese bureaucrats knew how to run Japan; they had been doing it for generations. Looking beyond the needs of the present, however, the Allied nations were determined to make Japan a true democracy. They wanted to continue the progress toward representative government that had begun with the Meiji Constitution of 1889, but had been slowed by the corruption of the 1920s and wiped out altogether by the military rule established during the war. They set up a committee of twenty-one Americans, four of them women, to write a constitution that the Diet could adopt as an "amendment" to the document given his people by the revered Emperor Meiji.

To no one's surprise, the new document had many resemblances to the United States Constitution and Bill of Rights. It stated that the authority of government comes from the people; the emperor is the *symbol* of the state. It guaranteed freedom of religion, of assembly and of thought.

It guaranteed the right to elect officials by secret ballot, and the right to a speedy and public trial. One of the committee, a young woman twenty-two years old, wrote an article guaranteeing equal rights for women. That was a new right in Japan, and one not yet guaranteed by the United States Constitution, but the article was adopted. There was also an article saying that Japan renounces forever the use of war as an instrument of policy, and that Japan would maintain no army, navy, or air force.

The hereditary House of Peers in the Diet was replaced by an elected House of Councillors. The House of Representatives was given more power to make laws, freed of its former close control by the executive branch. But the drafting committee kept the structure of prime minister and cabinet on European lines, from the Meiji Constitution. The cabinet can request the emperor to dissolve the Diet, in which case new elections are held. And the Diet can bring about the resignation of the cabinet by refusing to give to its policies a vote of confidence. The Diet adopted the new constitution in 1947.

The army and the navy were responsible for beginning the Pacific War and for losing it. The Japanese people were content to let the military men bear the guilt in whatever way they chose, including ritual suicide, while the rest of the nation put the war behind them and looked to the future. The Allied nations wanted more specific action. The Potsdam Declaration had stated that "stern justice shall be meted out to all war criminals, including those who have visited cruelties upon our prisoners." From May, 1946, to November, 1948, a tribunal of eleven judges from the Allied nations heard evidence against twenty-five national leaders accused of conspiring to wage aggressive war. General MacArthur declined Hirohito's offer to bear responsibility for all decisions in the war—trying him would have produced chaos in Japan. But Japan's wartime prime minister, General Tojo, was tried and, with six others, found guilty and executed. The other accused leaders were sentenced to prison. Seven hundred Japanese of lesser rank were also executed for individual acts of cruelty.

From the perspective of today, it is clear there were several reasons why thousands of Allied military men died while prisoners of the Japanese. Individual cruelty was one, coupled with samurai contempt for a fighting man who would allow himself to be captured alive. But another reason was the difference in the physical strength of the Japanese, hardened by months of arduous training to fight in the tropics, and the Allied personnel, rushed into war after short courses in how to fire a rifle. Long forced marches that the Japanese considered normal exhausted their prisoners. And in the final months of the war, food and medicines were in critically short supply for the Japanese and their prisoners alike.

Except for those being tried, Japan's five million men under arms were told to return to civilian life. More than half of them were overseas when the fighting stopped. The occupation organized a huge troop movement, using whatever ships were available, to bring them home. The ships also brought the Japanese civilians who had been working since before the war in Manchuria and Korea. All these people were available to work to rebuild Japan.

Rebuilding Japan meant more, of course, than simple construction of homes and factories. It meant providing an economic system that would enable eighty million Japanese to support themselves. American taxpayers were eager to have the expense of the occupation stop as soon as its goals could be accomplished. Two aspects of the Japanese economy needed changing, in the American view.

First, in 1945, forty percent of all the farmland in Japan was owned by landlords, who rented it to tenants for cultivation. Rents sometimes amounted to half of the crops grown. The occupation wanted the farmers to keep the income from their labor. At the insistence of the Americans, therefore, the government bought all farms larger than seven and a half acres and split them up for sale to farmers at low prices. The Japanese know how to tend land carefully so that it produces a lot of food. Better fertilizers and insecticides used after the war increased production still more. In a few years Japan supplied a greater proportion of her own food requirements than she had for decades.

Second, the occupation wanted to split up the great family financial empires in Japan—the zaibatsu. "Trust busting" had broken up the huge industrial combines in the United States long ago. Concentrations of economic power were considered undemocratic. Furthermore, the zaibatsu were accused of having led Japan down the path of conquest, as the Nazis and Fascists had led Germany and Italy. In truth, some of the zaibatsu had opposed the war and advocated peaceful trade as the best path to national growth. But it was difficult to convince the occupation of that. The Americans drew up a program requiring the great families to sell their stock in the corporations to the public and give up their posts as corporate officers. The program made slow progress. The sums involved were so huge the Japanese "public" simply did not have the money to buy ownership of the corporations. And the tradition of the wise senior adviser is so strong in Japan that the family heads set policy, whether they kept a corporate title or not. Nevertheless, as John Curtis Perry points out, "the upheaval of defeat, severe inflation, and a tax on capital did cause major redistribution of wealth in Japan," and new companies were founded and grew in the conditions of the postwar years.

It was obvious that Japan had to have industries if she was going to be self-supporting. The question facing the occupation planners was what kind of industries. Their first choice was textiles. Japan had been one of the three biggest producers of cloth in the prewar world. And textile plants are relatively inexpensive to set up. There was not much market anymore for silk, Japan's top prewar export, because of the introduction of synthetic fabrics. But the Japanese had also made cotton cloth of good quality. Lots of textile plants reopened in the 1940s.

Textile manufacture did not satisfy the Japanese for long. For one thing, their own silkworms had supplied the fiber for silk, but cotton fiber had to be imported. For another, textile mills needed semiskilled workers, and Japan had millions of skilled workers, including those who had come home from Manchuria and Korea. What was needed was industry that would allow those workers to transform a minimum amount of imported raw materials into products that would bring a good price on world markets. Cameras were an example. Before the war, the finest cameras were made by the Germans. Now Germany was in even worse shape than Japan, divided into zones for occupation by the Allies. The Japanese knew how to make cameras. They added some improvements made possible by wartime research, and soon Nikon and Canon cameras were rated with the best. Only so many people in the world appreciated and would pay for fine cameras, though. Japan's skilled workers needed to make products everybody wanted.

They found what they were looking for in electronics: tape recorders, small transistor radios, television, and stereophonic sound systems. All these sold especially well in the United States, where they soon dominated the market.

The next step in the development of the Japanese economy came not as a result of occupation planners' advice or Japanese initiative, but as a result of a falling out among Japan's conquerors. At the end of the war, the Soviet Union picked up again its campaign to convince the nations of the world that communism was the best political system. The United States of America vigorously objected to this Soviet effort, citing the benefits of capitalism. Each side freely claimed that its system was "democratic." Various countries in Europe saw problems in both communism and capitalism and were experimenting with forms of "modified capitalism," involv-

A composite photo of neon advertising signs in Toyko suggests the enormous vitality of Japan in the postwar era.

ing some government control over their economies. That pleased neither the Soviet Union nor the United States. American, British and French troops were occupying the western parts of defeated Germany. Soviet troops were occupying the eastern parts of Germany and also the countries in Eastern Europe that they had "liberated" from the Nazis. To ensure that the Eastern Europeans would be on the communist side in the political debate, the Soviet Union used its troops to shut off these countries from travel and trade with noncommunist countries. In March, 1946, Winston Churchill told an American audience, "An iron curtain has descended across the continent."

In Asia, the Soviets took even stronger actions in the territories where Japanese forces had been directed to surrender to Soviet commanders: in Manchuria and the northern half of Korea. In Korea they sponsored a definitely communist government of "North Korea." In Manchuria they turned over land and weapons not to Chiang Kai-shek but to the leader of the Chinese Communist Revolution, Mao Zedong. That put Mao well on his way toward winning control of all China.

The rapid expansion of Soviet influence, by means just short of war, alarmed the United States. Germany had expanded her influence in the 1930s by exerting pressure on other nations in what was called "cold war," as a prelude to World War II. Americans began to say that the Soviet Union and the United States were now fighting a new cold war. If the cold war got hot, a strong base of operations in Asia would be invaluable to the United States. The nation with the greatest potential for strength, even after all the destruction of the war, was still Japan. Her people had made good progress toward democracy, as the United States understood the term. They had an undoubted tradition of capitalism. The policy of the occupation shifted bit by bit from treating Japan as a defeated enemy to treating her as a strong potential ally against communism.

The Japanese recognized the change in policy and raised some questions. The new constitution stated that Japan renounced war forever. Many Japanese liked that statement very much, especially in view of the horror of atomic war. The Americans replied that it did not apply to self-defense and set up a "National Police Reserve," very like an army and later renamed a "Self-Defense Force." Self-defense required weapons, and weapons required steel. The United States proposed that Japan rebuild its steel industry.

At that point some Americans raised questions too. How could anyone be certain the steel would not be used someday against the United States? But the United States government, concentrating on "containing" communism, replied that Japan had to import the iron ore to make the steel. If worst came to worst, American naval control of the Pacific could always cut off the ore supply. So the Japanese economy added to its textiles and electronics a steel industry equipped with the most modern technology.

Importing iron ore required ships. And a steel industry had to sell its steel, either at home or by exporting it. The United States proposed that Japan rebuild her shipyards. The shipyards would buy the steel, and in time the ships they built could bring in the iron ore. So Japan built efficient modern shipyards and a new commercial fleet.

It took some years for these new industries to develop, of course. But they grew under very good conditions. The occupation continued its policy of working through the Japanese government, and the government had a long tradition of working as a partner with business leaders. American zeal for trust busting faded when it became apparent that the zaibatsu had the expertise and the organization to build the new industries. The new industries needed capital. The zaibatsu still had that, too. In the early postwar years the United States also sent aid to Japan amounting to nearly half a billion dollars annually, some for food but much for rebuilding. Later, as economic growth provided more jobs for the people, another tradition provided capital: the Japanese ordinarily put about twenty percent of their income into savings.

In 1950, Japan's economic growth got a big boost from an unwelcome source. The army of the new nation of North Korea marched south of the thirty-eighth parallel of latitude to try to take over the rest of the Korean peninsula. The United Nations Organization, or "UN," condemned this aggression, and the United States and sixteen other member nations sent an international "peacekeeping force" to Korea. The cold war had got hot. And, as expected, Japan was an invaluable base. She supplied harbors, airfields, food, repair services, cotton goods, electronics, steel and ships for the peacekeepers. When the troops needed hospital care, or just "rest and recreation" when on leave from their units, she supplied those too, admirably well.

Perhaps most important of all, "occupied Japan" supplied —or at least relinquished—a commander for the peacekeepers. It was General Douglas MacArthur, named Commander in Chief of the United Nations Command. MacArthur, now seventy years old, had little patience with such politicians' words as "peacekeeping mission." He knew a war when he saw one, and as he said later, the object of war is victory. As usual, he developed an audacious and surprising strategy for combat, and soon drove the North Korean invaders back across the thirty-eighth parallel. But when the UN troops crossed into North Korea, Mao Zedong sent vast numbers of Chinese soldiers to Korea. Their tactics, which they called "man-sea," involved not brilliant planning but sheer weight of numbers. Even MacArthur found the going slow against Mao's waves of men. He proposed that UN planes bomb Chinese military installations in Manchuria, the source of the Chinese troops. But other American military men, who were advising President Harry Truman in Washington, predicted that bombing Chinese territory would start World War III. The United States State Department also advised against the bombings. President Truman ordered MacArthur to limit the war to the Korean peninsula. Instead of accepting the order of the president, who is also Commander in Chief of United States military forces, MacArthur made several speeches in which he called for "total victory." Controversy broke out in the United States, and President Truman ordered MacArthur to make no more public statements on the matter. MacArthur spoke on, and for that act of insubordination President Truman relieved him of his command in April, 1951. The general returned to the United States. This incident made a profound impression on the Japanese by showing that the civilian head of the government is more powerful than any military man, no matter how brilliant, admired, and popular.

As a practical matter, the occupation of Japan really ended with the beginning of the Korean War, for most of the occupation troops were sent to Korea, and the attention of the occupying nations was diverted from Japan. MacArthur's successor, General Matthew Ridgeway, recognized that the departure of the American Caesar marked a turning point for Japan, and that the Japanese were ready to run their nation with much less advice from outsiders. The transformation from enemy to ally was complete.

In view of this situation, it was now time for an official peace treaty between Japan and the Allied nations. Such a treaty was signed by Japan and forty-eight of the Allied nations in September, 1951, in San Francisco. The Soviet Union refused to sign, but did sign a separate agreement with Japan in 1956. The treaty established the territory of Japan as the home islands and no more. On the day of the signing, Japan and the United States also signed a mutual security pact, which provided that United States forces would continue to be stationed in Japan to protect her from attack while she built up her own capacity for defense. The peace treaty took effect April 28, 1952. That marked the official end of the occupation.

12

Japan
a World Power

 Today Japan manufactures more automobiles than any other nation in the world. She is also number one in production of ships and television sets. In total value of goods and services produced, she ranks third among the nations, surpassed only by the United States of America and the Soviet Union. In 1945, Japan was a land in ruins, defeated, occupied by foreign troops. Her brilliant record of growth in the years since then has set analysts all over the world asking, "How did Japan do it?"

The Japanese of the second half of the twentieth century have many qualities that lead to success. Basic is the centuries-old tradition of hard work. Visitors who stay long enough to get to know the Japanese man in the street often comment on how hard he works, and how cheerfully. Related is a tradition of saving a good part of current income for the future —a willingness to do without some things today in order to have a better life tomorrow. Savings accounts of ordinary Japanese provide much of the capital needed for industrial growth.

Also, from the ancient life of Japan and from the words of Confucius, comes a sense that each individual is part of a group and that his or her life will improve as the life of the group improves. In samurai times villagers cooperated under the direction of a village "headman" to build rice paddies or defend the village. Today assembly-line workers cooperate under a foreman to meet their factory's quality standards.

Other characteristics that contribute to Japan's success are high levels of intelligence, skill, and literacy in her work force.

Outside influences have also played a large part in Japan's development, of course. Outside influences arrived in Japan in droves after World War II. Most important was the new constitution, largely written by Americans, which has given Japan a stable government that has encouraged growth. The Liberal Democratic Party has won enough seats in the House of Representatives in every election since 1955 to have the right to name the prime minister. The next largest party is the Socialists, who operate as a sort of permanent opposition. This arrangement provides a continuity of government policy that is a great help to the businessman who wants to make long-range plans.

A key provision of the constitution says Japan will have no army, navy or air force. The experience of the atomic bombs at Hiroshima and Nagasaki left most Japanese devoted to the pursuit of peace. And the mutual security pact between the United States and Japan, signed in 1952, promised protection from outside attack. Even today, when Japan has a small "self-defense force," her military expenses amount to only one percent of her gross national product. That means much less of her wealth goes to taxes to pay for the military than is the case in other industrialized nations. More of her wealth is available for economic growth.

In addition, just five years after World War II, in 1950, military expenditures of other nations began to benefit Japan. During the Korean War, purchases totaling four billion dollars for the United Nations military forces stimulated the Japanese economy to a growth that has continued ever since. By October, 1950, production in certain industries had risen to the level of prewar days. By 1955, Japanese production overall was equal to prewar, and the growth of several new industries was yet to come.

Japan's postwar industries were new in two senses. Because most of her industry had been destroyed by the war's bombing raids, she had to build new facilities. Naturally the new ones incorporated all the latest technology and were much more efficient and economical to operate than the old ones. Nations that had been spared bombing, like the United States, continued to use old facilities, with the result that these nations required many more hours of labor to produce a given product than Japan did. Japanese industry has raised the wages of its workers until now they are as high as those paid anywhere in the world, but because of the greater efficiency of the modern plants—and the diligence of the workers—total costs are less in Japan. In shipbuilding, for instance, costs are twenty to thirty percent less than in other countries. Japan has become the world's leading producer of huge tankers to carry oil.

Postwar industry was also new with regard to the products made. Some, such as transistor radios, had not been invented before the war. Others, such as automobiles, had been manufactured in Japan only on a small scale.

The first Japanese company to have its stock sold on the New York Stock Exchange was the electronic innovator, Sony. This company, founded after the war by Ibuka Masaru and Morita Akio, has become a worldwide enterprise by developing a long series of new products, each noteworthy for its high quality. Messrs. Ibuka and Morita were the first in

Morita Akio (above) and Ibuka Masaru founded the Sony Corporation to make tape recorders, soon after the war. One of Mr. Morita's most popular recent products is the Walkman cassette player. Today, as a transnational corporation, Sony manufactures and sells television sets, transistor radios, video recorders—and Walkman—all over the world.

Japan to make tape recorders. They were the first to make transistor radios. Their researchers developed a color picture tube for television superior to anything on the market. Now they are leading contenders for dominating the compact disk digital recording field. Their publicity people claim with much truth that they helped make the words "Made in Japan" a symbol for quality around the world. The Japanese have always appreciated quality in products. At times they have exported cheaply made goods because that was what they could sell in foreign markets. But customers in Japan insist on good design and durability and expect to pay for quality.

The greatest surprise in world markets was the Japanese motor vehicle industry, now the world's largest. Especially remarkable is the story of the Honda Motor Company, founded by a blacksmith's son who learned about cars as an apprentice in a Tokyo repair shop.

Honda Soichiro was born in 1906 in a village in southern

Honshu. He remembers well the first car that visited his village and how it appealed to him as a child fascinated by machinery. In time he opened his own repair shop, and then a factory to make piston rings. After World War II, he saw how much the Japanese needed transportation that would be inexpensive to buy and would use little gasoline. He began manufacturing motorbikes and motorcycles, which sold well in Japan and, before long, around the world. He then added trucks, sports cars, and finally family sedans to his Honda line. He was very successful in selling in the United States, joining the much older Japanese companies Toyota and Nissan in competing with Ford, General Motors, and Chrysler. In time the Japanese companies outsold the long-time top-selling import in the United States, the German Volkswagen. Honda's rapid rise demonstrates how much more open to new companies the postwar economic climate in Japan is, compared with the prewar domination by the zaibatsu.

In 1982, Japan had the capacity to produce twelve million cars each year. Japan's population of one hundred and twenty million buys about 5 million cars each year—a high rate of buying. That still leaves millions of cars to be sold abroad. The export peak, reached just before the economic recession of the early 1980s, was five million cars. In 1980, nearly two million were sold in the United States, a country whose products had long dominated the world automotive scene. Many were also sold in another great car country, Germany.

Competition from Japanese cars led United States and German manufacturers to ask their governments to set quotas to limit the number of units imported. Instead, the governments' diplomats requested the Japanese government to impose limits on the number of autos exported, and a voluntary agreement was reached.

On the Japanese side, the agreement was largely the work of one particular arm of the Japanese government, the Ministry for International Trade and Industry, abbreviated MITI. This powerful bureau, staffed by a corps of economic experts, advises leaders of both government and industry on desirable objectives for national growth—or in this case, national restraint. Advice from MITI over the years has been so good that industry usually follows its recommendations, even when it means losing an immediate advantage for the sake of a long-range goal. In Japan, industry and government work closely together, with government supplying capital for new ventures or expansion much more often than is the case in countries practicing complete free enterprise. This has led some frustrated businessmen from other countries to complain that they are competing not with individual companies but with one huge national corporation, which they have named "Japan, Inc."

Japan's remarkable achievement in economic growth attracts the most attention around the world. But she has had many other achievements in the postwar years, and of course some problems, too.

The health of the Japanese people has improved to such an extent that they now have the longest life expectancy of any nation on earth: eighty years for women and seventy-four for men. Improved nutrition has been increasing the average height of the people for several generations. This is particularly noticeable with today's Japanese teenagers. Between 1958 and 1978, the average height of fourteen-year-olds increased three and a half inches.

In 1964, Tokyo was host to the summer Olympic Games. Thousands of athletes, and more thousands of spectators, came to Japan from all over the world and were impressed with the nation's splendid modern stadiums and transportation facilities. In 1972, the winter Olympics were also held in Japan, on the snowy north island, Hokkaido. In 1970, the great port city of Osaka was the site of an international exposition, or "World's Fair," which served as a showplace for Japanese products and technology.

One of the most dazzling achievements of national tech-

Building superhighways in mountainous Japan is terribly expensive. But the Japanese buy five million cars every year, and they want roads. The fact that they spend very little on defense helps make such public works affordable.

nology at that time was the Bullet Train, a train that runs at maximum speeds over one hundred and thirty miles an hour on a specially constructed track between Tokyo and Osaka.

Even after buying all those automobiles, the Japanese still depend heavily on railroads—the mountainous terrain makes highway travel slow except on a few superhighways constructed at enormous expense. In 1966, work began on building the world's longest underwater tunnel to connect the islands of Honshu and Hokkaido. Development work is now underway on an even faster type of train, using a magnetic levitation propulsion system. In tests such a train has reached speeds over three hundred miles per hour.

Japanese have won Nobel Prizes in physics in 1949, 1965 and 1973, and in chemistry in 1981. In 1968, the novelist

The Bullet Train travels between Tokyo (below) and Osaka at maximum speeds of 130 miles per hour. An even newer type of train, using the force of magnetic levitation, has reached 300 miles per hour on a test track.

Kawabata Yasunari won the Nobel Prize for Literature for his novels *Thousand Cranes* and *Snow Country*. In 1974, former Prime Minister Sato Eisaku won the Nobel Peace Prize for leading the nation to pledge never to acquire nuclear arms.

Japanese woodblock prints continue to be popular in the West. Perhaps the Japanese art form best known in the West is the film, ranging from adventure epics like *The Seven Samurai* and *Shadow Warrior* to probing psychological dramas like *To Live* and *Ugetsu*.

Rapid growth like Japan's always brings accompanying problems. One of the most visible was serious pollution of water and air, caused by the many new factories and the increase in the number of automobiles. The Japanese soon faced that problem and passed laws requiring various pollution control devices. Air and water quality today is much better than it was a decade ago.

Another problem resulting from growth is more difficult to deal with: housing. As workers leave the farms for jobs in factories or service industries, the population of cities grows rapidly. Land in the center of cities is terribly expensive. Most office workers must choose between living in very crowded apartments close to their work, or traveling two hours each way to a small house and garden outside the city. Japanese industrial corporations often build complete housing developments for their employees. But even that is not an ideal solution for the housing problem: some observers point out that Japanese corporations already direct the work, the health care and the recreation of their employees, and company housing brings another large area of life under corporate supervision.

Corporate life puts stresses on family life anywhere, but especially so in Japan. The counterpart of the American expense-account lunch, where business is discussed, is the Japanese expense-account evening on the town. Many Japanese men go from the office to restaurants for long dinners with business associates, followed by visits to bars that continue far into the night. Executives of international companies are sent to work at branches overseas for periods of years, and not all can take their families with them. The result is that Japanese fathers may see much less of their wives and children than they would like and are under considerable strain as a result.

Japanese young people are also under strain because of the intense competition that exists throughout their educa-

Japanese children must learn to read and write the beautiful but difficult Chinese ideographs that are part of written Japanese. Competition for admission to the best universities is intense, so many parents begin pressuring their children to excel when they enter kindergarten.

tion. The best jobs go to graduates of Tokyo University. Therefore ambitious parents begin to prepare their children to get into that university when they are still in elementary school, sending them to extra classes on weekends and cram courses for admission exams. And since only a small percentage of applicants can be admitted to the top university, there are thousands who are rejected. Critics of the system say it is bad for everybody concerned—those admitted don't work at Tokyo University because they feel success in life is assured, and those not admitted don't work at other universities because they feel they are already doomed to be failures. That description exaggerates the facts, but the pressure is very real, and teenage depression is a genuine worry for the nation.

Yet another worry for Japan's leaders, today as in the past, is the inescapable fact that Japan is an island nation with a large population and very little farmland and very few natural resources of her own. Rich as Japan has become, she is in no way self-sufficient or independent.

In 1956, Japan won admission to the United Nations. Her leaders are determined that Japan will be a good member of the community of nations. The Japanese see more clearly than most peoples the necessity for continued international cooperation in a peaceful world, because their economy depends so much on international trade. In the 1980s, as in the 1930s, Japan imports raw materials and transforms them into goods which she sells abroad. In addition, eighty percent of the energy she uses comes from oil, which has to be imported.

Any threat to world peace, then, is a particular worry for the Japanese. They watch especially the situation in the Middle East, source of most of their oil, while working to develop other sources, including Alaska. They keep an eye on their two great neighbors on the continent of Asia, the People's Republic of China and the Union of Soviet Socialist Republics, and listen to their disputes. Someday, they hope, the lofty economic plans of those two nations' communist leaders will bear fruit, and trade will boom.

In the meantime, the chief trading partner of Japan is the United States of America. Japan buys and sells more there than in any other nation. And the United States buys and sells more in Japan than in any other nation except her neighbor Canada. This happy relationship has continued, despite occasional strains, since the end of World War II. It is the longest lasting, most successful relationship ever between an Eastern nation and a Western one.

Still, Japan is an Eastern nation, and it is in the East that she finds her brightest prospects for the future, as a leader of the developing nations of Asia. The plan of the 1930s to become master of Asia by conquest led to disaster for Japan. But World War II put an end to the Age of Colonialism. All the European colonies regained their independence and have been going their various ways with varying levels of success. Some have followed capitalist models, and some communist models. All need to develop industry to support their large populations. Without question, Japan is the most successful example, among all the non-Western nations, of the change from an agricultural to an industrial society. The others cannot ignore that fact. Peaceful trade with Japan will benefit them and Japan.

But while their neighbors are moving into the industrial age, the experts of MITI have been thinking about Japan's place in what economists call the "Post Industrial" age. In centuries past, in all countries, the crops grown by farmers were the principal source of wealth. Rice was the standard of value in Japan well into the nineteenth century. But the Industrial Revolution pushed agriculture into second place, and in developed nations, manufactured goods become the principal source of wealth. Now, in Japan, the United States and other advanced nations, the largest item in the gross national product is not manufactured goods but "services": the total spent for health care, insurance, banking, transportation, communications, education and the like. The invention that set off the Industrial Revolution was the steam engine. The invention that ushered in the Post Industrial Society is electronic data processing, by computer. Some people use the term the "Information Society" for the new age.

MITI has launched Japan on a two-part campaign for leadership. First, plans are in place for the entire nation to be connected to an electronic network that will provide in every home and office a set like a television set that can be used for banking, ordering merchandise, consulting libraries, even voting in elections. Second, funds are being poured into research to develop a supercomputer more powerful than any now in use in the West. Computer scientists call it a "fifth generation" computer, or an "artificial intelligence." The Japanese plan to perfect many features now under development in various countries, including the ability to understand spoken commands and reply in speech or writing—and all in the difficult Japanese language. Leadership in data processing, say those who still think in nationalistic rather than international terms, will make it certain that the twenty-first century will be "the Japanese century."

Others take a broader view. As Honda Soichiro expresses it, "Technology is a tool to serve mankind . . . . It is a matter for regret that some people today mistake the means for the end and have the wrong idea that scientific technology itself is their goal."

Artificial intelligence can be an aid to sharing of knowledge among all nations. Honda and other automobile manufacturers are now building plants in countries around the world, using their expertise to provide jobs and automobiles for people who have not had either. Sony is doing the same with electronic products. In the Post Industrial Age, that sort of transnational thinking can speed such new twenty-first century achievements as colonies in space, which some see as the best solution for many of our problems here on earth. The cooperation between nations required for such enterprises may be the best guarantee of the world peace the Japanese want so much.

Bibliography

Beasley, William G. *The Meiji Restoration*. Palo Alto, CA.: Stanford University Press, 1972

Beasley, William G. *The Modern History of Japan*. New York: Praeger, 1963

Benedict, Ruth. *The Chrysanthemum and the Sword: Patterns of Japanese Culture*. Boston: Houghton Mifflin, 1946

Borton, Hugh. *Japan's Modern Century from Perry to 1970*. 2nd edition. New York: Ronald Press, 1970

Boxer, C.L. *The Christian Century in Japan*. Second corrected edition. Berkeley, CA.: University of California Press, 1967

Christopher, Robert C. *The Japanese Mind: The Goliath Explained*. New York: *Linden Press* (Simon and Schuster) 1983

Coffey, Thomas M. *Imperial Tragedy: Japan in World War II: The First Days and the Last*. New York: World, 1970

Cooper, Michael, ed. *The Southern Barbarians*. Tokyo: Kodansha International, 1971

Cooper, Michael, ed. *They Came to Japan: An Anthology of European Reports on Japan 1543–1640*. London: Thames and Hudson, 1965

Elson, Robert T. and the Editors of Time-Life Books. *Prelude to War*. Alexandria, VA.: Time-Life Books, 1977

Gowen, Herbert H. *Five Foreigners in Japan*. Old Tappan, N.J.: Revell, 1936; and Freeport, N.Y.: Books for Libraries Press, 1963

Hall, John Whitney. *Japan: From Prehistory to Modern Times*. New York: Delacorte, 1970

Ienaga Saburo. *History of Japan,* sixth edition. Tokyo: Japan Travel Bureau, 1962

Leonard, Jonathan N. *Early Japan*. Alexandria, VA.: Time-Life Books, 1970

Lyons, Nick. *The Sony Vision*. New York: Crown, 1976

Manchester, William. *American Caesar: Douglas MacArthur 1880–1964*. Boston: Little Brown, 1978

Murdock, James. *A History of Japan*, three volumes. London: Kegan, Paul, 1925, 1926

Perry, John Curtis. *Beneath the Eagle's Wing*. New York: Dodd, Mead, 1980

Perry, Matthew Calbraith. *Narrative of the Expedition of an American Squadron to the China Sea and Japan,* compiled by Francis L. Hawks, abridged by Sidney Wallach. New York: Coward McCann, 1952

Prange, Gordon W. *At Dawn We Slept: The Untold Story of Pearl Harbor*. New York: McGraw Hill, 1981

Reischauer, Edwin O. *The Japanese*. Cambridge, MA.: Belknap Press, Harvard, 1977

Reischauer, Edwin O. *Japan, the Story of a Nation*. New York: Knopf, 1970

Roberts, John G. *Mitsui: Three Centuries of Japanese Business*. New York and Tokyo: Westerhill, 1973

Sanders, Sol. *Honda: The Man and His Machines*. Boston: Little, Brown, 1978

Sansom, Sir George. *A History of Japan*, vol. 2, 1334–1615; vol. 3, 1615–1867. Palo Alto, CA.: Stanford University Press, 1961, 1963

Steinberg, Rafael and the Editors of Time-Life Books. *Island Fighting*. Alexandria, VA.: Time-Life Books, 1978

Storry, Richard. *The Double Patriots*. Boston: Houghton Mifflin, 1957

Storry, Richard. *A History of Modern Japan*, revised. New York: Penguin, 1982

Tames, Richard. *Japan in the Twentieth Century*. London: Batsford, 1981

Thomson, James C., Jr., Peter W. Stanley and John Curtis Perry. *Sentimental Imperialists: The American Experience in East Asia*. New York: Harper and Row, 1981

Vogel, Ezra. *Japan as Number One*. Cambridge, MA.: Harvard University Press, 1979

Worswick, Clark. *Japan: Photographs 1854–1905*. New York: Pennwick/Knopf, 1979

Zich, Arthur and the Editors of Time-Life Books. *The Rising Sun*. Alexandria, VA.: Time-Life Books, 1977

Index